Praise for *The Boys of Dunbar*

"*Boys of Dunbar* is more than a book about basketball. At a deeper level, it's an inspiring tale about the magnificence of the human spirit played out in the lives of young people on and off the court. . . . A gem of a sports story."
—Bill Hughes, *Baltimore Times*

"[Danois's] tale of the basketball exploits of a handful of high school students in the 1980s shows young men motivated by their coach and other recreation leaders to dream beyond the hardship of their geography. . . . Expertly re-creates not only a season but the mood of a growing sport."
—Bijan C. Bayne, *The Washington Post*

"The numbers say everything about the magical run by the boys' basketball team of Baltimore's Dunbar High School in the 1981-82 and 1982-83 seasons. . . . Inspirational stories can be found everywhere in high school sports, but Dunbar and its legendary coach, Bob Wade, stand out for the sheer talent to converge at Dunbar those two seasons."
—*Booklist*

"Yes, *The Boys of Dunbar* is a book about high school basketball. But it is much more than that. . . . *The Boys of Dunbar* is a book about survival, a book about perseverance, a story about hard work and overcoming obstacles. . . . The courage, leadership, and drive are remarkable, and *The Boys of Dunbar* chronicles it from its beginning."
—Frank Valish, *Under the Radar*

"A feel good story that's timely as well as true."
—Glenn C. Altschuler, *The Florida Courier*

"Riveting . . . reveals the backstory of the greatest team in Baltimore high school basketball history through a series of unforgettable moments."
—Dean Smith, PressBoxOnline.com

"The book is about basketball, obviously, but it's also about family and determination and brotherhood and inspiration, making it just as interesting socially as it is from a basketball standpoint."
—Joel Brigham, Basketballinsiders.com

THE
BOYS
OF
DUNBAR

A STORY OF LOVE, HOPE,
AND BASKETBALL

ALEJANDRO
DANOIS

SIMON & SCHUSTER PAPERBACKS

New York   London   Toronto   Sydney   New Delhi

Simon & Schuster Paperbacks
An Imprint of Simon & Schuster, Inc.
1230 Avenue of the Americas
New York, NY 10020

First Simon & Schuster trade paperback edition September 2017

SIMON & SCHUSTER PAPERBACKS and colophon are
registered trademarks of Simon & Schuster, Inc.

For information about special discounts for bulk purchases,
please contact Simon & Schuster Special Sales at
1-866-506-1949 or business@simonandschuster.com.

The Simon & Schuster Speakers Bureau can bring authors to your
live event. For more information or to book an event contact the
Simon & Schuster Speakers Bureau at 1-866-248-3049
or visit our website at www.simonspeakers.com.

Interior design by Joy O'Meara

Manufactured in the United States of America

10 9 8 7 6 5 4 3 2 1

Library of Congress Cataloging-in-Publication Data is available.

ISBN 978-1-4516-6697-7
ISBN 978-1-4516-6698-4 (pbk)
ISBN 978-1-4516-6699-1 (ebook)

For Maia and Laila, thanks for the constant inspiration.

*For Mom and Dad, who always believed, supported,
and encouraged.*

*For Ericka, thanks for the music and laughter,
for being a wonderful mom to the girls, for your friendship
and, through everything, your love and push to do better.*

I like to hear of wealth and gold,
And El Doradoes in their glory;
I like for silks and satins bold
To sweep and rustle through a story.

The nightingale is sweet of song;
The rare exotic smells divinely;
And knightly men who stride along,
The role heroic carry finely.

But then, upon the other hand,
Our minds have got a way of running
To things that aren't quite so grand,
Which, maybe, we are best in shunning.

For some of us still like to see
The poor man in his dwelling narrow,
The hollyhock, the bumblebee,
The meadow lark, and chirping sparrow.

We like the man who soars and sings
With high and lofty inspiration;
But he who sings of common things
Shall always share our admiration.

Common Things, by Paul Laurence Dunbar

CONTENTS

CONTENTS

1981–1982 PAUL LAURENCE DUNBAR HIGH SCHOOL BASKETBALL ROSTER

Team Name: Poets
Mascot: Owl
Colors: Maroon, White, and Gold
School Address: 1400 Orleans Street, Baltimore, Maryland 21231
Assistant Coach: Lynn Badham
Head Coach: Robert P. Wade

NAME	POSITION	HEIGHT	YEAR
Tyrone "Muggsy" Bogues	Point Guard	5 foot 3	Junior
Gary Graham	Shooting Guard	6 foot 4	Senior
David "Gate" Wingate	Forward	6 foot 5	Senior
Reggie "Russ" Williams	Forward	6 foot 7	Junior
Tim Dawson	Center	6 foot 7	Junior
Reggie "Truck" Lewis	Forward/Center	6 foot 7	Junior
Darryl "OJ" Wood	Point Guard	5 foot 6	Junior
Jerry White	Forward	6 foot 3	Junior
Keith James	Guard/Forward	6 foot 4	Sophomore
Karl Wallace	Guard	5 foot 10	Senior
Keith Wallace	Guard	6 foot 1	Senior
Eric Green	Guard	6 foot 3	Junior
Ellis Dawson	Forward	6 foot 4	Senior
Kevin Amos	Guard	6 foot 2	Senior
Priestly Reeves	Forward	6 foot 5	Senior

PROLOGUE: "LIKE BROTHERS"

THE SEEDS OF THIS book took root on the playgrounds of Brooklyn, New York, in the early 1980s. A hoops fanatic, I spent countless mornings, afternoons, and evenings playing against my friends in the tilting, fenced-in concrete courts of the East New York, Bedford-Stuyvesant, Starrett City, Clinton Hill, and Fort Greene neighborhoods.

The steel rims were bent at oblique angles—slowly succumbing to years of violent dunks. The withered paint identifying the half-court, free-throw, and out-of-bounds lines had been rubbed raw by generations of abuse at the heels of rubber-soled sneakers.

In the frigid, early-winter mornings, when exhaling created a mirage of cotton clumps floating out of our mouths, my buddies and I shoveled the snow, ice, and slush that layered the courts to get a game going. On oppressively humid nights, we scattered from our apartments, like roaches at the flick of a light switch, into drenching downpours. The suction created by the wet elements allowed us to palm our favorite orange basketball, bald from years of fights against the unforgiving blacktop.

We stacked nickels earned from returning empty soda cans and purchased sets of tight netting, woven together in the patriotic ensemble of red, white, and blue. The nets dangled from the rims, like diamonds from the earlobes of a stunning woman. Cosmetics aside, the true reward was the sweeter than Kool-Aid sound of a perfect jump shot rippling through the twine before spinning back toward earth. Invariably, the nets would vanish in a day or two.

I imitated the ball-handling wizardry that was coded into the DNA of New York City point guards and dedicated many a solitary session to honing a jump shot that, I was sure, would lead me to Madison Square Garden and a lucrative contract with my New York Knicks.

On a few occasions, I shared the court behind my apartment building with my neighbor—a teenage man-child who was lustily pursued by the slick recruiters representing this country's premier institutions of Higher Basketball. He was a star at Brooklyn Technical High School, All-City, and on a direct flight out of the neighborhood, climbing onward and upward toward a shot at the NBA. I would rebound his missed shots, staring with reverence at his sparkling white Chuck Taylor Converse sneakers. I wondered if, one day, I, too, would be blessed with the same massive musculature that he packed onto his 6-foot-8 frame.

In 1983, that neighbor, Lorenzo Charles, would go on to author the most famous ending in NCAA Finals history. He rescued an air ball, propelled from a teammate's 30-foot desperation heave that had no discernible hope of touching rim. Somewhere between the Rio Grande and Sandia Mountains, in the game's waning moments, the ball floated down through the dry, hot, thin air of The Pit in Albuquerque, New Mexico, and landed softly in his outspread mitts. At the apex of his jump, Charles delivered a relatively bland two-handed dunk at the final buzzer that allowed Coach Jim Valvano's North Carolina State Wolfpack to defeat Clyde Drexler, Hakeem Olajuwon, and the heavily favored University of Houston Cougars by a score of 54–52 to capture the NCAA title. It was one of the biggest upsets in the history of sports.

The frantic scene of pandemonium at the conclusion of the 1983 championship game is the NCAA Tournament's signature moment, the visual definition and affirmation of the multibillion-dollar bonanza known as March Madness. The image of Valvano sprinting across the court—his tie flailing like Clark Kent's en route to a phone booth, his face blended into a cocktail of ecstasy, terror, shock, and deranged joy—has been a staple of CBS's television coverage, like syrup on pancakes, ever since.

My buddies and I passed many a day in the park, not only playing, but dissecting and debating any and everything hoops-related. One day, we went through the pantheon of legendary names produced on our home turf—the playground legends like the Destroyer, the Goat, Jumpin' Jackie Jackson, the Helicopter, Pee Wee Kirkland, and Fly Williams, acclaimed pros such as Kareem Abdul-Jabbar, Lenny Wilkens, Bob Cousy, Connie Hawkins, and Tiny Archibald. We followed the timeline up to our current favorites, Julius "Dr. J" Erving, Bernard and Albert King, Sidney Green, Sam Worthen, and Vinny "the Microwave" Johnson. We marveled at the teenagers we watched in high school and summer tournaments, or heard about in the tales of urban legend, like Dwayne "the Pearl" Washington, Lloyd "Sweet Pea" Daniels, Richie "the Animal" Adams, John "Spider" Salley, Ed Davender, Bruce Dalrymple, Rod Strickland, the Coney Island Marbury brothers Eric, Donnie Jr., and Norman (whose younger brother Stephon would go on to surpass them all), Chris Mullin, Mark Jackson, Walter Berry, and Ed Pinckney, who, we were certain, would one day add to the legacy.

A man in his young twenties, a neighbor with incredible talent whom we'd watched and cheered for in neighborhood hoops tournaments, resplendent in a burgundy silk sweat suit, gold medallion, and those funny-looking new sneakers called Nikes, listened intently, adding his own two cents on occasion. As he stood up, stretching a lithe 6-foot-4 frame, he looked at me with one raised eyebrow and said something I'll never forget.

"Yeah, New York is the king of basketball. But the best team I ever saw is from Baltimore," he said. "Dunbar! The dudes on the BENCH are going Division I on scholarship. They've got the number one high school player in the country named Reggie Williams. But the funny thing is, he's not even the best player on his own team. Their best player is the point guard, a little dude about five feet tall, a midget named Buggsy."

We laughed at that last statement, thinking he was joking. "Yeah right, a midget point guard named Buggsy? And he's better than the top player in the country? Okay." We giggled and shrugged.

Shortly thereafter, I was attending a prestigious boarding school in Massachusetts on a scholarship for talented minority students from the inner city. Initially homesick, I took solace in one facet from home, the one universal language spoken everywhere. I surrounded myself with it, insulating myself from a profound cultural shock wave. It carried me through five painstaking hours of study every night. I wasn't in Brooklyn anymore, but I still had basketball.

I quickly acclimated myself to Boston's subway system, "The T," and frequented the gyms at Harvard, Boston College, Northeastern, as well as the famed Boston Garden. Thanks to a classmate whose father had access to season tickets, I sat eight rows behind the Celtics bench. It was an incredible upgrade from my beloved nosebleeds in Madison Square Garden. I witnessed Red Auerbach light that damn victory cigar more times than I care to recount. I became enraptured by the steamy, decrepit structure that shook to its core as Larry Bird's soft jump shots splashed through the nets.

I saw a frail-looking, wiry kid named Reggie Lewis at Northeastern University annihilate the college competition and admired his skill and fearlessness. When I learned that he didn't start for his high school squad back in Baltimore, I wanted to find out about that team. Sure enough, he played for the Dunbar crew that I'd heard about in one of my playground debates back in Brooklyn.

I stayed glued to the new cable channel with the innovative idea of twenty-four-hour sports programming, ESPN, to the consternation of my prep school classmates. And when I saw an incredible, 5-foot-3 point guard at Wake Forest named Muggsy Bogues, a one-man fast break and defensive press, the likes of which had never been seen before, I damn near fell out of my chair. "That's Buggsy!" I screamed at the television in my dormitory's common room the first time I made the connection to the miniature point guard from Baltimore whom my neighbor had told me about. "Ayo, that's Buggsy!" My dorm mates, who did not seem to share my enthusiasm, looked at me with shreds of pity and amusement. I watched giddily as Muggsy assumed the role of David to the ACC's Goliaths.

I observed Gary Graham and Keith James playing for the University of Nevada at Las Vegas in the 1987 Final Four, and saw David Wingate and Reggie Williams win the 1985 national championship at the apogee of Georgetown University's reign atop college basketball. I followed the progression of the Dunbar Poet teammates, an astounding four of them who played pro ball, reading the box scores after every game. And I wondered about what their lives were like as kids, the relationships they had with one another, the individual and family struggles they overcame, what growing up in Baltimore was like, what happened to those who didn't make the pros, the ones who didn't play ball after college, and the ones who had their last hurrah as adolescents in high school.

———

This book, about the 1981–1982 Dunbar Poets—among the greatest high school basketball teams of all time—is a reminder of what the game was, and what it needs to become again. The '81–'82 Poets, with a plethora of top NCAA prospects and an astounding four team members who would go on to play in the NBA, grew up in a different time and place. It was a time when the head coach, Bob Wade, knew the players since they were kids, had grown up with their relatives, and was feared, in a loving, paternal sense, not only by his players and former players, but also by the criminal element that engulfed the struggling East Baltimore community.

The 1981–1982 Dunbar Poets had all the prerequisites of a great team. A great team is led by a great teacher and coach on the sidelines, and pushed by some alpha dog among them, whose personal example inspires and elevates those around him. Such a team has strong leadership from top to bottom. Pat Riley was one of the best coaches in NBA history, but it was Magic Johnson's leadership that stirred his Lakers teammates to play at a level that they would not have without his presence.

An outstanding team is much more than a collection of talented players. A great team shares the ball openly and willingly, and each member feels invested in the team's success. Every player must understand his role and perform it to the best of his ability. The team must work in unison.

A dominant team has a diverse set of weapons, enabling it to excel in a fast-paced, up-and-down game, or in one that is a grinding series of slow half-court offensive sets. It excels offensively and can suffocate an opponent on defense.

The players might not always get along, but they respect one another as teammates. They can communicate oftentimes without speaking, simply by observing one another's expression or body language. They have an emotional intelligence on top of their athleticism and technical prowess that allows them to compensate for one another when needed.

The Boys of Dunbar had these qualities. Many of them had known one another since they were toddlers. They'd played together on the same milk crates when they were too small to reach a ten-foot rim. They'd eaten at dinner tables with one another before they showed the potential to earn a college scholarship or have a shot at the pros. Their coach knew their families before they were even born. In a true sense of the word, they were a family.

The Dunbar players did not worry about how many shots they took or who grabbed the most rebounds. They believed in the family dynamic that Coach Wade taught. They knew that their skills were valued within the family and that those skills would lead to playing for a great college program and a free college education.

The mounds of recruiting mail, along with all of the celebrated and eminent college coaches, like North Carolina's Dean Smith,

Louisville's Denny Crum, Georgetown's John Thompson, and Maryland's Lefty Driesell, made their way to Coach Wade's office as the initial and most important point of contact in the early 1980s. The parents awaited Wade's approval before any school could make its recruiting pitch in the player's living room. As an educator who had played professional football and knew all too well the brutal nature of college and pro sports, Wade's priority was what was best for his players, not how much he could squeeze from Nike, Reebok, Adidas, and Pro-Keds, or the coaches and wealthy boosters from the nation's college hoops factories. The players, many of whom could have been *the* featured superstar at another school, loved one another like brothers, bonded by their neighborhood ties and desire to add to the Dunbar legacy. They played for the name on the front of the jersey, not their individual names on the back. During the off-seasons, they played together in local Baltimore tournaments called Project Survival or the BNBL (Baltimore Neighborhood Basketball League), events that held great meaning and prestige for them. They were not splintered off, traveling the country on competing AAU teams, fighting one another for prime recruiting position or rankings. The only national ranking that mattered to them was the number one ranking that Dunbar would eventually attain as the best high school team in the country.

When you examine the embarrassment of riches that Coach Bob Wade had at his disposal, on top of all of those important elements that great teams have, the level of talent that the Poets possessed is astounding. You can go position by position down to the last man on the bench and you will find the perfect high school team.

Reggie Williams was 6 foot 7, the nation's top player, who could play guard, forward, and center. He could shoot, rebound, defend, and block shots. How good was he? A year after leaving Dunbar, during his freshman season in college, he was the most outstanding player in the NCAA national championship game, helping to deliver the title to Georgetown University.

David Wingate was one of the best defensive players ever. He played in the NBA for fifteen years.

Reggie Lewis did not even start for the Poets and yet still went on to become the captain of the Boston Celtics.

Gary Graham was a captain on UNLV's 1986 Final Four team.

Tim Dawson was the Atlantic 10 Rookie of the Year at George Washington University before transferring to the University of Miami.

And Muggsy Bogues was an extraordinary talent, the shortest player ever in the NBA, a one-man fast break and defensive press who astounded everyone who watched him play, both in college and in the NBA. We'll see more Michael Jordans before we see another Muggsy Bogues.

Ten members of the Poets teams from 1981 through 1983 played major college basketball, four of them made it to the NBA, and three of those were first-round draft picks.

As young kids, they made a pact, promising one another to stay on the right path and avoid the pitfalls of their predecessors.

In high school, they complemented one another perfectly. They raised the spirits of a struggling city—grabbing the city of Baltimore's heart like no other team has, before or since—came together to inspire others, and set the table for Sam Cassell, Carmelo Anthony, Will Barton, and others who springboarded out of Baltimore into the NBA. And most important, they loved one another like brothers.

No recent high school player in Baltimore was more celebrated than former Patterson High School point guard Aquille Carr, a 5-foot-6, jet-quick, athletic marvel who was more popularly known by his nickname, "the Crimestopper," because city police noticed a sharp decline in activity on notorious drug corners whenever he played.

Carr's father, Alan, grew up in East Baltimore competing against the players who would comprise the great Dunbar teams of the early '80s. One of Aquille's role models is none other than Muggsy Bogues, who spoke with and counseled him on the pitfalls to avoid and the necessary skills to polish in order to succeed as a short player at the game's highest levels.

For the city championship game between Patterson and City College High Schools during Aquille's sophomore season, the Hill Field House on the campus of Morgan State University was filled to capacity, with five hundred fans stranded outside in subzero temperatures who could not gain admission. Carr, saddled with early foul trouble, sat on the bench for large portions of the first half. He erupted for 24 second-half points and led Patterson to a runaway 75–59 victory. He finished with 32 points, 8 assists, and 4 steals, with many of his spectacular plays causing pandemonium in the stands. Seated next to me, watching that game, was a woman in her seventies, Vivian Hockaday, who'd also seen the majority of the games played by the '81–'82 Dunbar Poets.

When Aquille dribbled and weaved through traffic like a human blur, delivering implausible passes that resulted in easy baskets for a teammate, eliciting earsplitting roars from the crowd, Miss Hockaday shook her head and laughed. She looked over at me with dancing eyes shielded by thick glasses and tapped me on the arm as I feverishly wrote in my notepad.

"We haven't seen anything like this since Muggsy," Hockaday said, nodding toward Aquille Carr. "But can you imagine him playing with four other guys who were just as good as he was? That's what it was like with those Dunbar teams back then. We'll never see anything like that again. My god!"

THE
BOYS
OF
DUNBAR

CHAPTER ONE

"Yes I Can!"

AT THE CONCLUSION OF the first varsity basketball practice for Baltimore's Paul Laurence Dunbar High School, the young men gathered in the gymnasium were exhausted.

They all stood at attention, varying shades of brown faces glistening with perspiration, staring at the bear of a man who'd alternated between screams of disgust and soft words of encouragement. They were the chosen ones, the few who had actually realized the dream this early in their lives. Through every summer tournament, winter recreation league game, and one-on-one contest, through every solitary morning sidestepping broken glass and empty liquor bottles, dribbling a ball through imaginary defenders to practice jump shots or master the backboard, the boys' goal was the same. Not the NCAA, not the NBA, but suiting up for the only franchise that mattered to them, Dunbar.

They yearned to hold aloft the flame of Dunbar basketball excellence. Whatever their drill sergeant of a coach demanded of them, they demanded of one another. The Dunbar tradition was a major source of pride to a large swath of the city of Baltimore. This fact was not lost on any of them.

The imposing edifice of Dunbar High School was stuffed tightly amid dreary housing projects and sagging row homes in predominantly black East Baltimore. For all of the drab building's shortcomings, the gymnasium inside was a veritable shrine, a sacrosanct place to the young men now standing on its hardwood floor. Despite their weary muscles, the boys were anxious to get their season under way.

For head coach Bob Wade, who was also Dunbar's head varsity football and baseball coach, and returning players like junior All-American Reggie Williams and highly recruited seniors David Wingate and Gary Graham, the disappointment of the previous season's 94–91 triple-overtime loss to Calvert Hall, a Catholic school, remained fresh in their minds. It was a contest that many thought was one of the greatest high school games ever played between two Baltimore area schools.

Despite the months that had passed and the fresh start that a new season promised, that loss inspired Dunbar from the first whistle of that initial practice. Wade was entering the season with a mind-boggling record of 132–10 as Dunbar's head coach, having won five Maryland Scholastic Association titles over the previous six years. But there were many people in the city who questioned his success and the tactics he employed to achieve such a sparkling résumé. There were whispers from parents and coaches at other city schools intimating that Wade recruited his players.

Two of his team's new starters had transferred from other schools at the beginning of the '81–'82 school year. Some people wanted an investigation and sanctions, referring to Dunbar as "the city All-Stars." But the truth, as difficult as it was for some to accept, was that Wade did not need to recruit. Dunbar was the city's marquee public school program, with an astounding talent pool that resided in the surrounding housing projects. Almost every talented kid in the city wanted to play there.

"I never recruited a player, nor did I have to," said Wade. "Dunbar had a tradition of excellence that many kids dreamed of being a part of. That tradition was established long before I ever got there. I was just lucky enough that so many talented kids wanted to be a part of what we were doing." Wade may not have "recruited" players, but he certainly singled out those youngsters he believed showed the most promise, regardless of their neighborhood or school district.

The Poets had lost three games the year before. Wade was more determined than ever that this new squad was going to do better. His challenge every year was to find which buttons to push with certain players; who could accept being yelled at and who needed quiet encouragement. At various points in practice, he joked, he cajoled, and sometimes he yelled and insulted. One minute, he'd appear surly, brusque, and dyspeptic, the next solicitous and benevolent. With the talent at his disposal, he drove them mercilessly, determined to make practices so difficult that every game, no matter who they faced, would be a cakewalk. In his eyes, the three losses that they had suffered the year before were three too many.

Wade emphasized the game's details, the subtle nuances that many high school kids never learn to master. His practices were filled with hours upon hours of drills that fostered a mastery of things like defensive footwork, swift defensive rotations designed to keep players between the opposing man and the basket, how to take charges, how to set screens, the proper angles to take when rolling off the screen and cutting to the basket, how to box out for rebounds, and how to throw outlet passes, among a plethora of other details that could be the difference between a win or a loss in a close game. Wade ran the same drills over and over again, programming his players to react quickly and correctly to various game situations. The casual fans who packed Dunbar's gym and didn't have an advanced understanding of the game undoubtedly enjoyed the frenetic pace that the Poets played at, the alley-oops, the slam dunks, and the way they ran the ball down an opponent's throat. They might have assumed that his players were just great athletes and that all Wade had to do was roll the ball out and let them run up and down the court. But sophisticated students of the game could see the discipline, how fundamentally sound and unselfish his Dunbar teams were, how they'd coalesced as a unit, always seeming to make the right plays by instantaneously adjusting.

Wade's other obsession was academics. From the mandatory study halls that were required for his players year-round, even when their sport was out of season, to the teachers he convinced to give up a slice of their free time to volunteer as tutors, Wade's commitment to his athletes' classroom responsibilities was un-questioned. If a star player needed help, Wade had a support infrastructure in place. He'd make sure his kids worked in the classroom because he knew that one day the balls would stop bouncing. If a star player failed, there were no special provisions or demands on teachers to let his boys slide by for the sake of athletic victories. If they couldn't handle their responsibilities in school, they simply couldn't play for him.

———

Wade also had another mechanism in place that allowed him to keep tabs on his players outside of the school: the neighborhood grapevine. He'd walked the same streets during his youth, knew

the neighborhood inside and out, and had a network of infor-
mants, from law enforcement personnel like his good friend Marshall Goodwin, who worked as an officer with the city's sheriff's
department and served as the team's de facto bodyguard, to folks
involved in the less desirable elements of the underground economy. Having grown up in the area, he was well respected, even by
the criminal element. Despite their illegal activities, even the drug
dealers operated by a tacit code in East Baltimore: Bob Wade's
Dunbar Poets were off-limits.

But the city's drug trade was metastasizing into something
far more malignant; its victims were being snared at an earlier
age than ever before. When Wade was a teenager, the heroin
trade, with its scarce supply and great demand, was run by old-
school traffickers whose inventories were, in effect, "regulated."
These were people who saw themselves as businessmen, who
kept their circles small. It was a matter of ethics for them to keep
the trade away from the street corners and the neighborhood
children. Their drugs were processed in safe houses and later
distributed through bars, pool halls, and nightclubs, or delivered
to individual customers in their apartments or private homes.
They had a conservative, long-term approach to their business
philosophies.

The old-school kingpins had enduring links to small local
businesses through legitimate investments and loans, where
they effectively washed their money. They nurtured community
support by giving away Thanksgiving meals to needy families,
purchasing and having groceries delivered to the elderly, sponsor-
ing bus trips to local amusement parks and neighborhood block
parties and picnics. But the demarcation of keeping kids away
from the narcotics trade was crossed in the late 1970s when a
new breed of kingpin emerged and changed the business model

in favor of swelling profit margins. The drugs moved out of the nightclub scene and into open-air markets. But perhaps their most treacherous attempt at modernization was the recruitment of kids to join the expanding workforce. And among the prime recruiting targets were the teenagers in the Lafayette Courts housing projects, where many of Wade's players had resided over the years.

When Wade was coaching in the early 1980s, cocaine experienced a phenomenal growth in popularity on the already battered streets of urban America. With the bountiful supply of cocaine available, enterprising teens began setting up their own shops, running back and forth via Greyhound bus or Amtrak trains to Upper Manhattan's Washington Heights neighborhood, where they could buy unlimited supplies of high-grade cocaine at wholesale prices. As the adolescent army and new breed of drug dealer flourished, they proved to be wantonly reckless and indiscriminately violent in settling turf wars with rival dealers for the prime drug market corners.

In addition to their fancy clothes, flashy cars, and sparkling jewelry, they also owned a stupefying amount of high-powered semiautomatic weapons. Where the teen gangs of Wade's East Baltimore were fighting with their hands or knives to settle who the toughest crew was, the teen gangs of East Baltimore in the 1980s were fighting with deadly assault weapons to control the multimillion-dollar narcotics trade. And the body count was becoming increasingly filled with innocent children and working folks who happened to get caught in the crossfire.

"The drug culture in Baltimore underwent a significant change with the emergence of a dealer by the name of Maurice 'Peanut' King in the late 1970s, whose rise was precipitated by a joint federal and city law enforcement task force that basically took down the older, major heroin dealers, one by one," said Sunni Khalid, a former crime reporter for the *Baltimore Sun*. "They thought they'd be able to dry up the market for heroin, but I-95, which ran right through the heart of Baltimore, was the East Coast's main drug corridor, and Peanut King simply filled the vacuum. But he changed the dynamic of the city's drug business philosophy because he took advantage of Maryland's lax juvenile justice system, employing teenagers to sell his drugs.

"This was at a time when Baltimore was deindustrializing. East Baltimore was a collection of blue-collar neighborhoods from the 1920s through the late 1970s and early '80s, but when the shipyards and steelyards started closing down, the neighborhoods and schools started falling into disrepair. These teenage drug dealers became their family's main wage earners. The proximity of the drugs drew closer to the schools and as cocaine moved in, you had guys like Peanut King reconfiguring the old drug territories, giving the responsibility on the retail level to this army of young, undisciplined, and uneducated kids. As the years progressed, the drug dealers became younger and younger.

"The Eastern District used to be the smallest of the city's nine police districts, only 3.1 square miles, but they started experiencing the highest number of drug-related shootings. The dealers were fighting for territories, and they were arming themselves with arsenals. AK-47 assault rifles started showing up on the streets, as did bulletproof vests. The open-air drug markets opened in the early 1980s and stayed open for business, twenty-four hours a day, for close to twenty years. So you had this erosion of respect for elders and any type of authority figures. The effects devastated the community, and the incarceration rates skyrocketed. The mothers, once the strength of the family unit, were now out in the streets chasing the cocaine and crack high.

"The local economy had broken down, the neighborhoods were being transformed for the worse, the good jobs dried up, and family units and schools broke down. It was all such a vicious cycle."

But while the street culture and mentality of the community were changing, Wade remained rigid in his adherence to old-school principles. One thing he would not tolerate on the basketball court was showboating. No one was ever allowed, after a great play or a victory, to thrust his pointer finger in the air, signifying that he was number one. The Poets were inculcated with the philosophy that to disrespect one's opponent was disrespectful to the game itself. If a player threw a behind-the-back pass where a simple chest or bounce pass would have sufficed, he found himself sitting on the bench shortly thereafter.

———

When the final school bell rang on that late autumn afternoon in 1981, the Dunbar players made their way to study hall. At exactly 3:30 p.m., study hall commenced, and the only sounds to be heard were the opening and closing of textbooks, the whirring of the ventilation system, and snippets of conversation from the adjacent corridors and stairwell.

Before anyone could practice, he was required to complete every homework assignment due the next day. Wade set no specified time to start practice; it came after study hall. Only after the homework was reviewed by one of the teachers who volunteered as tutors could players go to the gym. Practice began when the last textbook was closed.

"There are certain expectations that are placed on you as a player who wears the Dunbar uniform," Wade said, launching into his standard speech before commencing the inaugural practice of each season. "You should have been working out on your own, and if you haven't, we'll soon find out. It's not going to be easy. Because of who we are, there is a target that will always be on your back. In order to deal with that, day in and day out, we will go that extra mile. No one will be more prepared and in better condition than we will. No one has invented a pill that you can swallow to get you in the kind of shape that you need to be in. It starts right here."

He spoke as if he were reciting items on a grocery list, but Wade was still burning on the inside at how the previous season had ended. He was eager to begin again. Although there were many recent additions to the team and personalities that needed to be incorporated into his system, he liked what he saw early on. This team had size, speed, and quickness. They were tough and looked hungry.

He blew his whistle, and the players strapped on the sand-filled backpacks that sat at their feet. They then scooped up two bricks, one for each hand, and a seemingly endless number of full-court sprints followed. Then, to half-court and back followed by suicide runs—sprints to the nearest free-throw line and back to the baseline, followed immediately by a sprint to the half-court line and back to the baseline, with an ensuing sprint to the free-throw line at the other end of the court and back to the baseline, concluded by a full-court dash to the far baseline and back.

The players were then separated into small groups and instructed to continuously jump as high as they could, with the bricks extended over their heads, up and down and up and down, for twenty minutes straight. Next were agility drills, defensive footwork and step-slides, quick dashes to certain spots on the court and swiveling on a dime, knees bent, arms outstretched while sliding and pivoting around the floor.

Then senior guard Gary Graham dropped a brick. As soon as it hit the ground, Graham smiled at the collective groan of his teammates. At the sound of the whistle, the torturous regimen began again. Sprints, suicides, jumping and agility drills, footwork. When finished, the players removed one another's backpacks—with bricks still in hand. Then the routine started again. Then they started yet again, this time without the bricks. And only when that was done, were the balls rolled out and the passing drills begun. They ran through their offensive and defensive sets, as well as the various full-court and half-court press alignments that they would be implementing in more detail over the next few weeks. It would be hours before a single shot was taken, before they finally segued into fast-break drills, along with half-court and full-court scrimmages. At the final whistle, some four hours after practice had begun, they came to a halt in front of Wade.

Despite their fatigue at the end of that first practice, the players listened intently as they gathered around their coach. Wade was, undeniably, the boss. For the newcomers—even though they had been warned by the veterans—the intensity of the practice was a shock.

Among those struggling to stand was 5-foot-3 junior point guard Tyrone Bogues. It was his first official practice as a Dunbar Poet and he, of all the team's new players, should not have been surprised by the intensity of the workout. He'd been watching Dunbar practice since he was a little kid. Yet he was astonished. Watching the team practice for years was one thing; experiencing the brutality of Wade's practice was quite another. Wade had long been eyeing Muggsy and his childhood friend Reggie Williams. The Lafayette Recreation Center, which was a short walk from Dunbar and where the boys grew up playing the game, was almost a farm system for Wade's teams. Wade knew that Bogues, despite his tiny stature, and the tall, slim Williams were rare talents. He'd been studying their development since middle school, while also allowing them the privilege of watching his teams' closed-door practices.

Wade would also have open-gym sessions during the fall, spring, and summer, where neighborhood youth could come in to play pickup games on the hallowed court. This wasn't done with any charitable purpose in mind. Wade knew the power that the Dunbar brand carried in the community. He also knew that the neighborhood's best players who weren't of high school age would be there.

"When we were kids, we would love to play in those pickup games on Dunbar's court," said Bogues. "Coach Wade would be in his office, and we'd be playing as hard as we could. We were hoping that he would notice us. That's all we ever talked and dreamed about growing up: playing together at Dunbar for Mr. Wade."

At the start of each new season, Wade would walk past Bogues and Williams, who were watching practices, and ask them the same question, "How many years until you guys are going to be playing for me?" And while the length of Williams's arms and legs grew over the years as the countdown proceeded, Bogues never did grow much, though over time he began to look like a miniature bodybuilder.

"All we cared about as kids was wearing that maroon-and-gold uniform for Dunbar when we got to high school," said Williams. "In elementary school, we'd sit up in the stands going crazy like everybody else. We knew all of the team chants and all the words to the team songs and cheers that the cheerleaders would do. We felt like we were part of the team, like we were part of the

Dunbar family. Mr. Wade made sure that we would get into the games for free. But it wasn't like he did that because he knew we would one day grow up to become great players. We were in elementary school, so he didn't know what type of players we would grow up to be. The older guys from the projects that played for him would tell him, 'Hey, Coach, Muggs and Russ [Williams's nickname] are pretty good,' and he'd just smile and look at us and say, 'Okay, we'll see one day.' But it was beyond basketball; he was interested in us as kids because you have to understand that our parents, uncles, and siblings had all gone to Dunbar. He knew my parents, he knew Muggsy's parents, and he knew people in our families before we were even born."

In addition to his stellar accomplishments in the city's youth basketball leagues, Bogues was a phenomenal Ping-Pong player who possessed an incredibly fast set of hands and superior eye-hand coordination that couldn't be taught. He was also an outstanding youth wrestler whose aggressive mauling of opponents was legendary.

"When I wrestled, I didn't have to worry about the short jokes and being too small, which is what I heard all the time when I played basketball," said Bogues. "But despite what everybody was saying, I always believed in my basketball abilities. My mother didn't know much about basketball when I was a kid. And she really didn't come to see me play. But when I would tell her about the negative things people were saying and how they doubted me, she always said, 'Don't worry about it. No one can be an expert on your life. They don't know how big your heart is, and they don't know what you're capable of. Keep doing what you want to do.'"

It was Elaine Bogues who kept the family together after her husband, Richard "Billy" Bogues, was arrested on an armed robbery charge when Tyrone was twelve. Billy was sentenced to a twenty-year federal prison term, which he served at the correctional facility in Jessup, Maryland. Prior to Billy's incarceration, Tyrone, his brothers, and sister thought their dad's sole job was working as a stevedore, unloading the cargo of the massive steamships in Baltimore's ports. But they soon learned that Billy didn't spend all of those irregular hours and days away from home solely working at the docks.

"Whenever we asked where he was, our mom always said that he was out working, and we never had any reason to think otherwise," said Bogues. "I remember piling in the car as a family, going to drive-in movies or the beach or amusement parks, just having fun. We would love to sit down with my mother on the weekends while she watched her favorite kung fu movies and westerns. But I also remember that my dad was out of the house a lot. When he got locked up, I started to understand that when he wasn't home, he was getting into some things he shouldn't have. He was selling drugs, committing armed robberies and stickups, living a life on the streets that he eventually paid for."

Bogues would harbor a resentment against his father for years. As he later said, "I was so mad at him, but I didn't know how to release it." After a few trips to see his father in prison, Bogues stopped visiting him until his college years.

Having depended on Billy financially, Elaine was forced to go on public assistance when he was incarcerated. She immediately went back to night school and earned her high school equivalency, working alongside her oldest son, Chucky, who was also there finishing up his studies. Tyrone watched his mom work menial jobs during the day, go to school at night, and study whenever she could. Elaine eventually would secure full-time employment as a secretary at the Kennedy Krieger Institute, a renowned medical and psychiatric institution that worked to improve the lives of children with developmental and behavioral disorders. With her extended family and older siblings chipping in when times got hard, she managed to keep the bustling household afloat.

Whenever he stepped on a basketball court, Muggsy played with a sense of purpose, determination, and hunger that was incomparable. When he got to Dunbar, the derisive voices of people mocking his chances of succeeding at an elite level pushed him even harder. There was also something else that propelled him every day, a frightening circumstance that had taken place eleven years prior that few knew about. It would continue to motivate him for the remainder of his life.

——

The sun was setting on the east side of Baltimore on an early autumn weekend in 1970. At 1115 Orleans Street, a squat, red-brick, low-rise building like countless others in the Lafayette Courts housing projects, five-year-old Tyrone Curtis Bogues had just come down to the living room from the upstairs bedroom he shared with his two older brothers in the family apartment.

Built fifteen years earlier, Lafayette Courts rose out of the ashes of blocks of dilapidated row houses, 550 units, that had been bulldozed in a massive slum clearance to make room for eleven 105-foot-tall, high-rise towers and a host of surrounding two- and three-story low-rise buildings. It was an urban renewal project that aimed to house 807 families in what would become, at the time, 1952, the nation's largest housing project outside of Chicago.

When the first towers were raised, instead of extolling the views of the nearby harbor that they offered, a reporter for the *Baltimore Sun* newspaper, in a bit of foreshadowing, focused on the chain-link fencing that enclosed the outdoor corridors and its concrete floors, comparing them to a well-kept prison. But early residents of Lafayette, before the plague of Baltimore's stupefying drug problem and its attendant violence crept into the homes and lives of the average person, recalled the area to be wholesome, neat, and comfortable. It was a place where neighbors would look after one another in an extended-family village, courtyards awash with joyful sounds of children's games, as opposed to what would come later—the frightful screams of residents scampering to evade the whizzing bullets, as warring drug dealers sought to settle conflicts.

But before the heroin and cocaine became widespread, before the buildings of Lafayette began to sag, before teenage drug dealers took over the stairwells, hallways, and outdoor courtyards, the neighborhood was a place where one could sit outside on warm evenings and snuggle in the comforting blanket of a caring community. Despite many of its residents living close to or below the poverty line, it was a place of shared dreams along with the frustration of the daily urban struggle, a place where kids didn't necessarily feel they were poor in a hamlet that did its best to take care of everyone.

In 1970, when Tyrone Bogues was five years old, Lafayette was somewhere between what it had been and what it would become. From his upstairs bedroom window, Tyrone could see a large crowd gathering on Orleans Street, where a man and a woman were screaming at each other. A crowd, composed mostly of kids and young teens, along with a few curious adults, grew quickly.

Ty, as he was known to family and neighbors, dashed downstairs to see firsthand what everyone else was so eager to witness. It was only a few quick steps through a light rain before he joined the crowd, his darting eyes trying to make sense of the situation. He immediately spotted Sherron, his eleven-year-old sister who doted on him and refused to let him out of her sight whenever they were outside together. Sherron was the one who would take little Ty over to the Lafayette Recreation Center around the corner, the one he'd follow like a puppy, watching, studying, and trying to emulate as she ran circles around the neighborhood boys while playing sports.

Sidling up to Sherron on Orleans Street, Ty also noticed his thirteen-year-old brother Chucky. As the buzz and chatter elevated, the man arguing with his girlfriend ran a few short steps, grabbed something off the concrete sidewalk, and in one fluid motion, stood up clutching a brick. Screaming, in a rage, he lifted it above his head, leaned back, and hurled it into Mr. Chester's soul food restaurant storefront window. The sound of the brick punching through the glass echoed through the air and floated above the traffic.

Mr. Chester's establishment was one of several small enterprises that lined Orleans Street, directly across from the northern lip of Lafayette Courts. The proprietors of these businesses—like the New Store, where kids would ruin their teeth with cheap candy and ice cream; Mr. Buddy's Barber Shop; Mr. Lou's Liquor Store; Mr. Fats Penny Store, where you strolled in to grab some tasty cookies; and Miss Mickey's and Mr. Ron's, which served up grilled steak or cold-cut sandwiches—were fixtures in the community who were all well known to everyone. These entrepreneurs and enterprises were small cogs in the local economy, as much a part of the fabric of the lives of Lafayette residents as the larger neighboring shops in the nearby Old Town Market. Residents from all over the city took the trolley to put a few dollars on layaway for some of the latest fashions at Diplomats, which everybody simply called "Dips," or to buy furniture at Epstein's. But Lafayette residents mostly patronized the local stores like Mr. Chester's.

"Old Man Chester," with a healthy head of black hair that belied his age, was an ornery sort. So when the crowd saw him burst out of his store wearing his customary blue slacks, plaid shirt, and easy-walker moccasins, they could see his bad intentions.

When they heard the brick-throwing perpetrator point across the street and say, "It was those kids!" the gawking crowd quickly began to disperse. The infuriated old man darted into a shed in the adjacent alley. When he returned seconds later, he was pumping and aiming his double-barreled shotgun at those still standing around. Little Ty, Sherron, and everyone else, now terrified, crouched and sprinted away from Orleans Street toward Lafayette's maze of walkways and alleys. Sherron was holding her baby brother's hand as they began to run. And that's when Mr. Chester, mean, old, and incensed, started firing.

Running through a small patch of grass in a neighbor's front yard, Ty lost his footing in a stretch of watery mud and fell to the ground. Almost immediately, a neighbor named Ricky dashed out of his front door and picked up the little boy to get him out of harm's way. Standing erect, before he could gather a head of steam to run to safety, Ricky dropped Ty the instant that shotgun pellets tore into his thigh. Back in the mud, and realizing that Ricky had been shot, Ty quickly jumped back on his feet and made it no more than a step or two before scattering buckshot ripped into his tiny arms, thighs, shins, and calves, sending him back to the ground in a heap next to a nearby fence that he'd hoped to scale.

"I had his hand when we started running," said Sherron. "Everything happened so fast, I don't remember letting go of his hand, and I thought he was still next to me. I didn't know what happened until people started screaming, 'Ty got shot! Ty got shot!' I saw him lying there, bleeding, and everybody was hysterical. Mr. Chester stopped shooting, and I ran over to my brother. There was all this blood. I thought he was going to die. People were running to get my mother. She came out, and while the ambulance was coming, the police were spreading out, asking us what happened. They'd already taken Mr. Chester away. He was lucky that the cops got to him first, because when our father and his friends showed up, it looked like they were ready to kill him."

The doctors at Johns Hopkins Hospital told his family that the little boy was lucky that he hadn't been shot in the face or head. He was also extremely fortunate that the shotgun had been loaded with pellets as opposed to the deadlier slugs, which he would have been unable to walk away from. Most of the pellets were removed from his body, but a few were lodged too deeply for the physicians to remove. Bogues would have to walk around with them for the rest of his life.

"Ever since that day, something happened inside of me," said Bogues. "It's hard to explain, but even as a little kid, getting shot, thinking I might die, and surviving, that gave me an inner strength. I felt like I could survive anything. I had this will, even back then, that if I wanted something, if I set my mind to something, I was going to work as hard as I could to get it. I wasn't going to sit around, be scared, or not do anything. In the back of my mind, I knew that I could've been dead, that I was lucky."

Bogues decided, after coming home from the hospital, that he wanted to achieve things. He wanted to be great at something. Coming from where he did, seeing the things that happened to people that he knew, he realized that life could be over in an instant. He took a vow that he wouldn't let anything stand in his way.

"I had this belief in myself, this inner confidence, from the day that I got shot, as crazy as it might sound, that I could do anything that I set my mind to," Bogues said.

CHAPTER TWO

"How You Doin', Baby?"

BOGUES'S EXPERIENCES AS A middle school wrestling champion and Ping-Pong savant sharpened his defensive skills on the hardwood. He enjoyed crowding his opponent from the moment he received an inbounds pass, hounding and muscling him as he attempted to dribble downcourt. It was a skill he absorbed through conversations with an older friend and neighborhood role model, Dwayne Wood, a 5-foot-6 point guard at Dunbar in the late 1970s who was considered at the time the city's greatest diminutive player.

Wood was an uncle of one of Bogues's best friends, Darryl Wood, whom everyone called "OJ," because he was such a big fan of the University of Southern California's Heisman Trophy–winning running back O. J. Simpson. But OJ and Dwayne lived in the same house and were more like brothers because they were very close in age. Bogues and his buddies would sit atop the Dunbar bleachers to watch Wood and his backcourt mate, Kevin Bush, another electrifying short player, wreak havoc against some of the city's best teams and players. The duo of Bush and Wood was coached by Bob Wade. They were known as "the Mighty Mites." Watching their speed, defensive intensity, uncanny passing ability, and knack for stealing the ball and creating chaos against opposing teams inspired Bogues. Dwayne Wood's constant encouragement and words of motivation were invaluable to him, and Wood never shied away from obliging his young protégé, who perpetually seemed to be bugging him for a game of one-on-one.

"I didn't watch a lot of college or pro ball back then," said Bogues. "But I loved watching Dwayne Wood play at Dunbar. He taught me how to use my size as an advantage, how to get up underneath players on defense and apply pressure to make them uncomfortable when they were dribbling. He taught me—contrary to the short jokes and people saying that I was too small—that with a certain knowledge, skill set, and aggression, that my size was a weapon."

But Wood's greatest contribution, outside of teaching him how a short, smart point guard could be effective, might have been anointing him with his childhood nickname. While observing Bogues, the smallest player on the floor, dominating his opponents and stealing the ball from everyone when he was about ten years old, Wood yelled out, "Hey, Ty, you're out there mugging everybody like that guy on the Bowery Boys!" Bogues walked out of that game with the nickname that stuck from that day forward, Muggsy.

"I didn't like that nickname at first," said Bogues. "I thought it made me sound like a criminal. But when I would steal the ball and the guys would start yelling 'Muggsy,' I started to like it because it was a sign of respect. Plus, there wasn't anything I could do about the name, whether I liked it or not, because in Baltimore, once you get a nickname that sticks, it's stuck for life."

Wade was fully aware that Bogues was the piece missing from the previous year, when his team had lost that triple-overtime game to Calvert Hall for the unofficial city title. As Dunbar walked off the court after that heartbreaking loss, Wade actually locked eyes with Muggsy, who was sitting in the stands. They had an understanding in that one brief moment that the game's outcome would have been different had Bogues been wearing a Poets uniform.

But a new school zoning system had recently been implemented that dictated Muggsy would spend his tenth-grade year at Southern High School. At the time, Baltimore's middle schools were composed of grades seven through nine, with high schools encompassing the tenth through twelfth grades.

Muggsy spent his freshman year at Southern, taking two city buses to school. When his family learned that he'd been zoned to attend Southern, they immediately set out to have him transferred to Dunbar, where his parents, uncles, cousins, and siblings had all attended. But his middle school records had been misplaced and weren't located until after the transfer deadline had passed. The rumor was that someone working in the school administration with a rooting interest against the Poets intentionally hid his transcript, effectively keeping him away from Dunbar's basketball team as an incoming tenth grader.

"I was furious and heartbroken that I had to attend Southern for my entire tenth-grade year," said Bogues. "All of my best friends that I'd grown up playing basketball with were going to Dunbar. My brother played there, my sister played there, my whole family went there. Southern was a bad school with a bad team. That was a very difficult year, watching Dunbar play, knowing that I should've been playing with them. That really hurt me."

"Muggsy's mom nicknamed us Mutt and Jeff because we were always together," said Reggie Williams. "I lived in the high-rise projects in Lafayette and he lived in the low-rise, and either I was at his house or he was at mine all the time. When he had to spend that first year at Southern, that was difficult. We talked about how we had to just get through that one year and then we'd be back together again on the court, but it hurt. I know it hurt him more than anybody else, but that year that he was at Southern, it wasn't as fulfilling a year as it could have been, because we knew that he should have been at Dunbar with us. And if he was, we all felt we would have been unstoppable, because that's how good Muggsy was."

At the beginning of the following year, Muggsy transferred to Dunbar from Southern. The Baltimore public high schools allowed students to transfer anywhere in the system to pursue a course of study that wasn't offered at schools they were attending. Dunbar offered courses in nursing and dental technology that weren't available anywhere else. Claiming to be fascinated by teeth, the city's best basketball players transferred to Dunbar unencumbered.

Resigned to the fact that he wouldn't be able to transfer until the next year, Bogues was ambivalent about playing basketball for the first time in his young life. While most of Southern's returning players, along with the hopefuls who'd be auditioning for the varsity, were participating in preseason conditioning drills in the fall, Bogues elected to focus on his grades so that nothing would impede his planned transfer the next year. Southern's head coach, Meredith Smith, wasn't pleased with Bogues's absence from his team's conditioning program. When official tryouts commenced, Smith read aloud the names of twenty players whom he deemed worthy of auditioning for the available varsity roster spots. When Bogues didn't hear his name, he looked at Smith quizzically.

"I had a big reputation throughout the city because of what I'd done in the recreation leagues growing up," said Bogues. "There was a lot of talk, all over the city, of how my skills would translate at the next level. There was a lot of anticipation about what Reggie Williams and I would do once we got to high school. Coach Smitty knew who I was, but I guess he was trying to assert his authority. But he had the wrong guy."

Even the returning varsity players were flabbergasted as they pleaded with Smith. "Coach, you forgot Muggsy. What about Muggsy?" they implored.

"I remember Smitty looking at me and saying, 'Naw, I didn't forget anybody. These are the guys that need to practice with this team,'" said Bogues. "I felt like showing something that day, so I went out and played with the JV team for that first practice. And I absolutely destroyed everybody. And then I didn't show up for another practice after that."

When Southern got off to a dreadful start, winning only one game with close to a third of the season already gone, Smith personally appealed to Muggsy and invited him to play. With a sprinkle of anger and self-professed immaturity, Bogues was adamant that he'd wait it out and just play at Dunbar the next year. But while he was playing in a winter recreation league and obliterating the competition, his mentor, Leon Howard, the director of the Lafayette Recreation Center, who'd been coaching and encouraging him since he first began playing, urged him to put aside his differences with Coach Smith so he could get some varsity experience before transferring to Dunbar. Howard insisted that getting a feel for the high school game would make for a smoother transition that next year.

———

Leon Howard had no idea that he'd one day wind up in Baltimore. Shortly after he graduated from college, he was working as a draftsman for General Dynamics in his home state of Connecticut, assisting the engineers in making changes to blueprints of new submarine projects. Four years into the job, a friend's uncle, after learning that Howard's degree was in physical education, asked him if he'd be interested in working in recreation.

Howard, who was becoming increasingly restless with the repetitive daily routine of his life, became intrigued at the thought of getting paid to work with and teach young kids, especially through sports. His friend's uncle told him that he had a friend in Baltimore who was a supervisor at the city's Department of Recreation and Parks. Howard immediately sent a letter to the department, which invited him to come to the city to fill out some paperwork and sit for an interview. In 1967, he drove from his home in Connecticut, a five-hour trip, and filled out an application. He drove home that same evening.

"Two weeks went by and I didn't think I'd get it," said Howard. "But I soon received a letter telling me I'd got the job and to come on down to Baltimore."

He stuffed all his belongings into his sparkling, forest-green 1966 Pontiac GTO, drove back to Baltimore, and began working right away. He was soon assigned to the Greenmount Rec Center on Greenmount Avenue, where he started as the center's director. Howard secured a map of Baltimore, and in his free time, drove around the city to acclimate himself to his new surroundings.

He loved his new job, enjoyed working with young people, and felt as if he'd found his calling. And he quickly established his reputation not only as a gregarious guy and an effective mentor to neighborhood kids, but also as a serious man who stood his ground. Within his first few days at Greenmount, he noticed that his staff seemed apprehensive about dealing with one particular teenager. The boy refused to listen to anyone, was mean to his peers, and intimidated kids and adults. After asking around, Howard learned that the boy came from a feared neighborhood family of older brothers and uncles whose calling cards were drug dealing and brutal violence. Howard tried to give him a fair shake, but when he heard that the boy was repeatedly riding his bike around the center and shrugging off the staff directives to stop, he decided it was time to step in.

"I told him, 'Look here, boy, you can't be riding that bike around in this building. If I see or hear about you doing it again, you *and* the bike are getting tossed in the street,'" said Howard. "A few minutes later, I saw him riding that damn bike in the center again. And he had the nerve to have a smile on his face."

After leisurely walking to a strategic position, and just as the obstinate offender attempted to speed past, Howard floored him with a forearm that sent the kid flying off the bike and crashing to the floor with a resounding thud, which drew gasps from the kids and staff who witnessed it. The instant the kid hit the floor, Howard calmly picked up the bike and walked out of the center's entrance with it. Limping, the youngster hobbled out of the center, screaming that his brothers and uncles would be coming back. Howard walked to the edge of the sidewalk, lifted the bike above his head, and tossed it into the middle of Greenmount Avenue.

"The staff was scared and asked me, 'Do you know who that boy's family is?'" said Howard. "They were nervous that his uncles and brothers would come back and raise all kinds of hell. I said, 'I don't give a shit who his family is! This is my center.' And nobody from his family ever did come to the center to say anything about it. I'm guessing they were tired of his little bad ass, too."

When he returned from a two-week military reserves commitment in the summer of 1967, Howard was informed that the city had transferred him over to the Lafayette Projects to run their recreation center.

"I was pissed," said Howard. "I said, 'Man! I don't know where no Lafayette is.' I had to get my map out and find my way over there. Little did I know that I would find a home, that I would find my calling."

No one could have predicted what Howard would do in terms of developing the potential of young athletes growing up in Lafayette.

———

Bogues always followed Howard's advice and reluctantly joined the Southern squad toward the end of the season. In his first game, he didn't start. But once Southern fell behind, Smith sent Bogues into the game. And for the rest of the season, he never came back out.

"I took over, and we became a totally different team," said Bogues. "I was putting up some strong numbers, both scoring and passing, and we wound up winning most of the rest of our games."

In one contest against a very strong Lake Clifton team, Southern was down by 5 points late in the game. Bogues stole the ball from a Lake Clifton player and passed it ahead to his teammate for an easy layup. Down by 3, he stole the ball again and assisted on another basket. Losing by 1 point with about twenty seconds left in the game, he again stole the ball and hit a teammate who was in perfect position near the basket.

"And he misses the layup! We wound up losing by one point," said Bogues.

Despite finishing the season at Southern, Bogues still felt as if he were part of the Dunbar team and attended as many of their games as he could. His friends would longingly look up at him in the stands.

"When they lost to Calvert Hall in triple overtime, they were actually winning by nine points with less than two minutes to play in regulation," said Bogues. "When it was over, Coach Wade walked off the floor, looked at me, and shrugged. Both Coach Wade and I knew that the only thing they were missing was a pure point guard, a playmaker who could make that team go. And I was that missing piece."

So Muggsy, like many other elite Baltimore ballers, caught the nursing and dentistry bug.

———

Although Dunbar was located in one of the most economically depressed and violent neighborhoods in the country, in the fall of 1981 the atmosphere inside of the building was cathartic. Despite the brutality and disarray on the streets, if a young person was serious about receiving a high school education, Dunbar provided that opportunity. The principal, Mrs. Julia B. Woodland, a product of Baltimore City Public Schools, had received her master's degree in education from New York University and another master's degree, from Johns Hopkins University, in mathematics. Walking briskly through the hallways during the school day, she called every student "Baby."

She knew and supported practically every young person at Dunbar, ricocheting around the building as if in a pinball machine, her head on a constant swivel as she addressed each young student in her path, constantly chattering, "Hey, baby! How you doin', baby? Baby, what did I tell you about wearing that hat inside? How's that math class coming, baby? Your mother called me this morning, baby. You having any problems, baby? Baby, let's get together and work this thing out!"

"Mrs. Woodland had the ability to motivate all of her students to go a step further than they normally would have," said Wade. "She was very firm, but she was also very fair. And she made sure that the surrounding community was an integral part of the school community."

During her tenure, the school building remained open seven days a week, oftentimes until ten at night, so that neighborhood residents, not just students, could access the swimming pool, theater, gymnasium, industrial shop, and other resources.

"The trouble with education is that it's been cut away from the community," Woodland had said in a 1978 interview with the *Baltimore Sun*. "That lets the school pass the buck to the parent and the parent pass the buck to the school. At Dunbar, we're trying to give the school back to the community. One way is to bring the community into the school."

"Every day, she would tell the students to repeat, 'Yes I can!'" said Wade. "She insisted that we use the phrase 'student-athlete,' and she demanded they be students first, students who took their academics seriously."

Standing 5 foot 7 and extremely articulate with a distinct, scratchy voice, she was a towering figure to every student at Dunbar during her tenure as principal from 1974 to 1984. *Baltimore Sun* reporter Michael Olesker once wrote that Woodland "had a voice like a blunt instrument across the frontal lobes . . . She wanted these kids to not only believe in themselves, but to believe there was a place for them in the American mainstream once their school days were behind them."

One of her proudest moments at Dunbar was traveling with the student choir to Rome, where they performed in front of the Pope.

She didn't refer to the young people who attended the school as her students; she called them, "my children."

"I have a rule," she was fond of saying. "If you do anything within a hundred miles of this school that's wrong, I'm gonna find out. And if you make the six o'clock news, it better be good news."

She often preached that her students—her "children"—had important responsibilities in life that began in Dunbar's classrooms. She told them that simply showing up was the biggest part of the battle, and that they could make a difference despite their own misgivings that the larger societal system was against them.

"Mrs. Woodland reminded me of those 1930s or '40s women that you would see on television," said Reggie Williams. "She was always in a nice suit, and her hair and her makeup was always done up. She had such a strong presence. We all called her 'Momma Woodland.' When she walked into a room, she owned it. She was smart, charismatic, and knew her sports better than most men."

Firm with the Poets star athletes, she constantly reminded them about their predecessors who'd dreamed of becoming big stars but hadn't made it. She'd tell them, "Everybody can't all make it. And what happens if you don't? Where will you go? What will you do?"

She attended most games during the season, but she was far from enamored with sports. Lefty Driesell, the head basketball coach at the University of Maryland, learned this firsthand. He'd once shown up at Dunbar at the start of a school year to speak with some of the more talented members of the Poets squad, only to be told by Woodland, "Get the hell outta here! This is only September. Don't start bothering my children now. You at least wait until the season starts."

Regardless of the destructive forces laying siege to the city's poor neighborhoods—swelling unemployment, ruthless brutality, a stupefying incarceration rate, horrible housing conditions, a rising tide of bloodshed and homicide exacerbated by a worsening drug epidemic—Mrs. Woodland's school was filled with hope. Her pleasant demeanor notwithstanding, she, like Bob Wade, was in total control. They might have been teaching in the middle of a war zone, but Mrs. Woodland and her staff came to work every day to prepare their kids to be productive in life. The teachers and support staff, along with Mrs. Woodland and Coach Wade, stressed hard work and achievement. They were people who grew up participating in the civil rights movement, passionate educators who were personally familiar with Jim Crow segregation, voter suppression, marginalized economic opportunity, and second-class citizenship. They were men and women who had fought and marched. They told stories about the struggle for black achievement, not from a lesson plan or textbook, but from their own experiences. These were people who cared, who genuinely wanted the next generation to reach higher and achieve what they, and their parents before them, had fought for. And more.

––––

Despite his stature, Bogues was a splendid floor general who orchestrated a frenetic, furious attack, shredding through opposing teams at an intense speed while always remaining under control. He ran an offense to perfection and handed out more assists than the local soup kitchen. But his worth to a basketball team was much more than simply outrunning the other team and delivering excellent passes to his teammates.

On the defensive end, he was a menace, singlehandedly disrupting another team's offense by mercilessly harassing and stealing the ball from their ball handlers. He was a double-double machine, not in points and rebounds or assists, but in assists and steals.

"I would watch my man, study him, set him up with different moves, read and time his dribble so I could steal the ball whenever I wanted to," said Bogues. "He'd be so worried about me getting steals and embarrassing him that it would take a toll through the course of a game. I would take his attention away from running his offense, making him play hesitant and worried, which took precious seconds off the clock. I always knew that I could never just play a normal game because if I did, I'd just be a liability because of my size. I was fortunate to love every aspect of helping my team win and understanding that there is so much more to the game than simply scoring that ultimately makes the difference between winning and losing. And I hated to lose."

Although his friends and Coach Wade knew how unique and special his talent was, Bogues was still an unknown commodity on the larger high school basketball landscape. But his best friend, Reggie Williams, was not. A 6-foot-7 forward whose nickname was "Russ," because he looked exactly like one of his uncles nicknamed Russ, Williams had given a transcendent performance at the prestigious Five-Star Basketball Camp in Pennsylvania over the summer. Run by the legendary Howard Garfinkel, this summer camp featured the best of the nation's top high school players and was a recruiting destination for all the country's elite college coaches. Garfinkel, or "Garf" as he was popularly known, was, at the time, the most powerful man in high school basketball before the sneaker companies and AAU began to exert the massive influence they now enjoy. Garfinkel was a shrewd evaluator of talent whose player ratings carried instant credibility.

Against his talented peer group, which included such future stars as Len Bias, Dwayne "Pearl" Washington, Chris Mullin, Mark Jackson, Johnny Dawkins, Tommy Amaker, and Brad Daugherty, Williams impressed Garf. Wiry, with long arms and catlike quickness, Williams had a great assortment of shots from twenty feet and in. He was also extremely crafty around the basket. An adroit rebounder, he possessed deceptive strength and an incredible basketball IQ.

Williams was a hesitant convert to the sport of basketball. He spent his early years growing up in the Pimlico neighborhood, where the Preakness Stakes, one of the three races in thoroughbred racing's Triple Crown, is annually held at Pimlico Race Course. His father had worked in the same warehouse as a laborer since he was a teenager and, when Williams was younger, his mother had been employed as a hospital orderly. When his parents separated, he lived briefly with his grandmother in the Douglass Homes in West Baltimore, where he developed a love for baseball and harbored dreams of being a Major League pitcher. When his mother, Gloria, eventually moved him, his sister, and two younger brothers into Lafayette Courts, he'd never actually played basketball before.

"My mom got sick and eventually had to stop working at her job," said Williams. "She went on public assistance. When we lived in Lafayette, I don't know how she made it work, being able to take care of her four kids like that, but she did. There wasn't much money coming in, but if I needed something, I always had it. She made sure that I had nice clothes on my back. We never missed a meal, and my mother was an outstanding cook."

His father, Melvin Williams, was not responsible for Reggie's height. He was stocky and stood 5 foot 10. But despite their differences in size and build, Reggie did inherit his father's personality.

"He was very dependable, very consistent, was always on time, and never missed a day of work," said Williams. "His personality was very similar to mine. He was quiet and stayed to himself. He was a man of few words, but he loved his Baltimore sports teams. He didn't say, 'I love you,' or express his emotions openly. My parents had separated for a long time before they got back together, so I didn't have a lot of interactions with him, but we bonded through sports, which we both loved."

Melvin rooted for the Baltimore Colts, but he absolutely loved the city's pro baseball team, the Orioles.

"He called them 'The Birds,' and whenever they came on TV, he was in his favorite spot on the couch, drinking his beer, watching them play," said Reggie. "In some households, fathers and sons do a lot of things together. It wasn't like that in my house. Men of that generation were tough, hard workers who provided for their family, but some of them just didn't know how to show love."

Their meaningful father and son conversations were about college football and NCAA basketball, the Bullets, or the Colts and the Orioles. But Reggie didn't need his father to hug him and verbalize his love.

"My father would never tell me he was coming to my basketball games when I was in high school, but he showed up at every home game at Dunbar and sat right behind the bench," said Williams. "And afterward, he'd never tell me that I had a good or a bad game. But it meant a lot to me when I would see him there. That's how he showed me that he cared."

Despite being so slender, Williams possessed a huge appetite. The family never went out to eat, and when one of his friends mentioned that he'd gone to a restaurant, Williams's response was, "What the hell is that?" He might have gotten something to eat from the 7-Eleven or the local McDonald's, but every family meal was eaten in their Lafayette Courts apartment.

"Whatever struggles my mom was going through on a day-to-day basis, I didn't really realize it because she never made it seem like the burden she was carrying was so heavy," said Williams.

His uncles loved watching the NBA's Baltimore Bullets games on television, and they'd take little Reggie with them to the playgrounds and recreation centers. But he was content to simply sit on the sidelines and watch. As a young child, he actually hated to watch basketball on television. He'd cry as his uncles watched the Bullets games, begging them to change the channel so he could watch one of his favorite shows. But once he began playing hoops, which was around the time that the NBA merged with the ABA, he grew to love watching those Bullets games on TV. His favorite player was the Philadelphia 76ers' incredible star Julius Erving, more commonly known by his nickname, Dr. J.

At Lafayette Courts, Williams met Muggsy Bogues. They became fast friends, always in each other's apartments.

"Out of the twenty-four hours in a day, I probably spent close to sixteen of those, every day, with Reggie when we were growing up," said Bogues. "He was very quiet around most people, but when he was with the fellas, he was funny and loved to laugh. He would crack his little jokes and sometimes, if he got started, you couldn't shut him up."

Once they became close friends, Williams and Bogues would refer to each other affectionately as Little Fella and Big Fella.

"Muggsy and I, and some of our other friends like OJ, would run over to the recreation center and pretend we were Dr. J, World B. Free, George McGinnis, Henry Bibby, and Doug Collins," said Williams. "We knew all those guys because it seemed like Philly was on TV all the time. And once I started playing, I couldn't stop."

Williams would bend a hanger into a rim, attach it to his bedroom door, and play late into the night with a little ball. He'd shoot it off the walls, dunk it, and bounce that ball all over the apartment.

"I know it drove my mother crazy, but she saw that it made me happy, so she would just say, 'Let the boy go ahead,'" said Williams.

Williams's skills developed rapidly after he first started playing organized ball, and he was quickly recognized as one of the city's top players in his age group. Most people assumed that he was painfully shy, while some thought he might have had a speech problem because he seldom talked. To those who didn't know him, he came off as a silent, uncommunicative, and apathetic introvert. But at home, and among his friends, where he felt most comfortable, he was outgoing and funny. While many people wondered about the skinny kid who barely talked, his friends were privy to his penchant for cursing.

——

But Williams was not the only member of the Dunbar team who was viewed as one of America's best high school players. Senior David Wingate, like Williams, was one of the most highly recruited players in the country. An elastic 6-foot-5 guard/forward with catlike reflexes, he could soar to the rim with tenacity and play hellacious defense. He could handle the ball with both hands and was an offensive threat anywhere on the court. He was representative of the new breed of talent populating the rosters of powerful college programs. Still learning the nuances of the game, he could sprint down the court at warp speed with the fluidity of a ballet dancer. Wingate, or Gate, as he was known, ran the wing and played the transition game with the sort of ferocity and athleticism being popularized at the time by future NBA Hall of

Famer Clyde Drexler and his college team, the fraternal order of Phi Slama Jama at the University of Houston.

Wingate used his bursts of speed to anticipate and jump the passing lanes. In the open court, he was a runaway train. His defensive prowess and steals helped initiate the Poets' vaunted fast break, which often ended in backboard-shivering, thunderous dunks.

Wingate was another youngster like Reggie Williams who, before falling under the trance of basketball, had dreamed of becoming a Major League Baseball pitcher. His parents had moved to Baltimore many years earlier from Florence, South Carolina, in search of the elusive American dream. Wingate's mother had only a fourth-grade education. His dad didn't go any further than the sixth, but hoped that the blue-collar wages up north could help him provide a better life and future for his loved ones. The baby of the family, David enjoyed opportunities that his siblings, most of whom were fifteen or more years older than he, did not. The siblings helped spoil him with baseball bats, mitts, uniforms, and other equipment. He would step on the playgrounds and occasionally shoot hoops for fun, but his friends always got the better of him. Basketball just wasn't his game, he figured, even though his older brother was known as one of the city's top up-and-coming players. One day, his best friend, Keith Wallace, convinced him to hop on the bus to take a ride and try out for the basketball team at the Cecil Kirk Recreation Center, where he was unceremoniously cut.

"I was always tall for my age, and my friends were all smaller than me," Wingate said. "They would joke on me for not coming out to the basketball court. When I finally got the nerve to try out for the thirteen-and-under team at Cecil Kirk, I got cut, even though I was the tallest kid there. My guys laughed at me during the whole bus ride back home."

Over the next year, Wingate kept growing and began playing more basketball with his brother Spencer, who was two years older and would go on to play at the University of Maryland, Baltimore County, and later as a professional in Europe. Spencer encouraged David, insisting that, though still clumsy, he was getting better.

"Spencer kept telling me, 'Man! You gotta start getting into this basketball!'" said Wingate. "I started playing with him and the guys from the neighborhood more and more. We built a court on a tree, nailed it in, used a piece of cardboard for a rim, and would play all day long out in a back alley."

The next year, his friends took him back to the Cecil Kirk Rec Center, where he made the team. But more important, Wingate came under the mentorship of two neighborhood coaches, Calvin Dodson and Anthony "Dudie" Lewis.

"Dudie and Dodson would come and pick me up, and I was getting better, but I still wasn't good," said Wingate. "But those guys put a lot of time into me. They were able to do things with me that my parents weren't. If it wasn't for Keith Wallace, who took me down there, and Dudie and Dodson, I would never have become the player that I eventually did. Those guys were so important in our lives. They knew all of the guys in the neighborhood who were big-time criminals and drug dealers, because they helped those guys when they were growing up, too. So long as they knew that we were playing ball and that we had a chance to go to college one day and accomplish some things, the drug dealers would look out for us as well."

It was an unspoken code of the unforgiving street life. Those involved in the criminal world might have had some fearsome reputations, but they weren't perpetually heartless and cold-blooded, especially when it came to the younger kids in the neighborhood.

"It was like, as long as we were doing something positive, they would help us out, give us a few dollars from time to time, nothing major," said Wingate. "On the outside, they might have been seen as criminals, but they never tried to exert any negative influence on me. It was always a situation where, if they knew you had talent and had a chance to do something in life, they would give you a pass, take an interest in you, and look out for you."

When he started to blossom into a formidable player around fourteen and fifteen years of age, Wingate began to notice why the environment during some of the city's recreation league games was a little bit more intense than it probably should have been. The neighborhood drug dealers would be there tossing big wads of money around as they bet on the games. Wingate would sometimes walk out of the gym with fifty dollars in his pocket, courtesy of a happy dealer who'd just won a big bet.

"Shoot, fifty dollars back then, to a fourteen-year-old kid, man, that was a whole lot of money," said Wingate. "I'd run out and buy some new Chuck Taylor sneakers and still have some spending money left over."

By the time he transferred to Dunbar High School after his tenth-grade year at Northern High School, at the urging of his coaches at Cecil Kirk, Wingate found that not only could he keep up with all of the kids who were once better than him, but he could also now dominate them.

In addition to David Wingate and Reggie Williams, Gary Graham was another member of the Dunbar roster during the 1981–1982 season who was being courted by some of the country's top colleges. Graham was a senior who also had come up through the Cecil Kirk Recreation Center. He was a defensive predator who devoured the opposition's top scorers. At 6 foot 4, he could take it to the rim strong, handle the ball, and deliver subtle, precise entry passes to a big man posting up close to the rim. But Graham's role was to linger far away on the perimeter and loft his accurate jump shots. Graham had played out of position as a point guard at times during the previous season, but now that Bogues was on the team, he would be back to playing his natural shooting guard spot.

Graham was the youngest brother of Ernie Graham, considered one of Baltimore's greatest players ever. A 6-foot-7, versatile scoring machine, Ernie was Wade's first elite player whom college recruiters fawned over. Ernie Graham began to bring some national attention to the young coach and his talented teams. Ernie had just finished his career at the University of Maryland (where he set the school record for the most points scored by an individual player in a single game) as Gary was looking to escape from his older brother's immense shadow and make a name for himself at Dunbar.

Wingate and Graham's former teammate from the Cecil Kirk Recreation Center program, Reggie Lewis, who went by the nickname Truck, was another recent transfer from Baltimore's Patterson High School. Lewis, along with the others, listened intently to his new coach's instruction on that first day of practice at Dunbar in 1981. Truck's reticent demeanor hid his raging desire to prove that he was one of the city's best players. Talented but raw around the edges, he owned a great set of hands and an unrelenting work ethic. Shy and introverted, the unpolished 6-foot-7 youngster was a silent assassin on the court. He'd operated in the shadows of his more heralded teammates and adversaries in Baltimore's recreation leagues from the day he slipped on his first uniform.

Lewis loved playing football and baseball growing up and came with much hesitation to the sport of basketball. His sister's boyfriend was a basketball junkie who traveled throughout the city looking for the best pickup games. He corralled the tall, slender boy and taught him defensive techniques, how to pass and handle the ball, as well as the art of boxing out opponents for rebounds. The boyfriend was an aggressive player who exposed Lewis to the mentality of the physical brand of hoops demanded on Baltimore's blacktops. The slight Lewis was pushed around at the start, but he learned to push back. What the friend did not have to teach was a gift already coded into Lewis's DNA. He was a pure, if unorthodox, shooter and scorer.

Other team members of the 1981–82 Dunbar Poets squad included Jerry White, a 6-foot-3 role player, and Darryl Wood, the soft-spoken, 5-foot-6 backup point guard whose nickname was OJ. Both of them had grown up in the Lafayette Courts projects with Muggsy and Reggie Williams. The four of them had been playing together for a long time. Wood was reserved and calm. His cheerful smile lit up any room that he walked into. Jerry White had the unfortunate distinction of being the younger brother of Barry Scott, a legendary former Poet. Scott was Coach Wade's first Dunbar player to receive a basketball scholarship to attend Georgetown University a few years earlier.

"Barry Scott was an incredible basketball player," said Wade. "He was extremely talented, very much similar to a guy like Reggie Williams. He was set to go to Georgetown and had a very bright future ahead of him."

Promises of easy, illicit cash from unscrupulous street agents, however, persuaded Scott to renege on his Georgetown commitment in favor of a college in the Northwest. A month after leaving for Idaho, he wound up at Compton Community College in Los Angeles before boarding a bus a few weeks later for Baltimore, with a few packs of peanut butter crackers in his pockets. He never played a game of college basketball and was found murdered, lying in a gutter, two years later. His death devastated Bob

Wade, who from that moment began a crusade against street agents and the shady side of college basketball recruiting. For everyone outside Dunbar, Jerry White was known only as the brother of the late, great Barry Scott.

"I became very bitter about what happened to Barry," said Wade. "He worked so hard to get the opportunity for that Georgetown scholarship, and he was swayed by the quick money and the street agents to go elsewhere. That made me become extremely protective of my players from then on, especially during the recruiting process. I became overprotective. I wanted to know who they were hanging out with, who was calling their house, who they were playing for in the summer. I wanted all of the recruiting to run through me, and I made it very clear to the street agents what would happen if they crossed the line with another one of my players."

On more than one occasion, Wade sent word to a neighborhood drug dealer or someone acting as a runner for a college coach, ordering them to back off. And the community stepped in as well.

"Barry's death affected the whole East Baltimore community," said Wade. "People were heartbroken and angry. They tried to help, and I'd get phone calls from people to report that they'd seen some of my players hanging out somewhere they didn't belong, or they were in the street when they should have been in school, or they were with someone they shouldn't have been with. I'd go straight to that player's parents, tell them what I'd heard, and let them know that we needed to work together because their kid was hanging out and becoming involved with a bad element."

Tim Dawson, a recent transfer from Towson Catholic High School and an excellent student, would patrol the center position for the '81–'82 Dunbar Poets. Standing 6-foot-7, he was a tenacious shot blocker, an excellent leaper with broad shoulders, long arms, and a solid, muscular build. Dawson flourished around the basket, devouring rebounds. No one was better at gathering the ball, recoiling instantaneously, and springing skyward to score on ferocious dunks.

Also gathered around Coach Wade, waiting to be released from that first boot camp practice was Keith James, the team's lone sophomore. His older brothers, Frank, whose nickname was Spoon, and Karl, played on some of Wade's earlier Dunbar teams and had both gone on to play their college ball at the University of Nevada, Las Vegas. Keith, like the two Reggies, was another quiet soul and a lanky, prolific shooter. He was everything that Wade loved in a player—an excellent defender, great in transition, unselfish, and a role player who never complained.

Going into the 1981–82 season, Calvert Hall, the private Catholic school that had defeated Dunbar the prior season, was rated by *Street & Smith's* and *Basketball Weekly* magazines as the best high school team in the country. No one had any idea what the boys of Dunbar were about to unleash on the nation's high school basketball scene. But Bob Wade had an inkling. He smiled upon dismissing his shell-shocked team after their initial practice, watching as the Poets walked gingerly out of the gym.

CHAPTER THREE

"Tension in the Air"

DURING THE FIRST FEW Dunbar practices of the 1981–1982 season, there was a feeling-out process among the players. There were still some lingering rivalries from their days competing against one another in the recreation centers. As the team's new point guard, Muggsy seemed to favor getting the ball to the guys he grew up playing with at Lafayette.

"There was still a little bit of tension in the air with the guys who came from the Cecil Kirk program and the guys who came from Lafayette," said the senior David Wingate.

Wingate was convinced that Muggsy was looking to pass the ball only to Reggie Williams and some of his other friends whom he'd grown up with.

"I could understand how the new guys felt that Muggsy was freezing them out during the first set of practices," said Williams, the team's marquee All-American. "We just had a chemistry that went back for years. We were instinctively connected. Those guys had to work their way into the mix. But there was also a little bit of, 'Hey, we're from Lafayette Projects. Ya'll are from Cecil Kirk, so you have to earn your stripes around here.'"

Within a few days, Wingate realized that he didn't have to worry about Muggsy freezing him out any longer, that if he ran and hustled and got out on the wing and was where he needed to be, his new point guard would get him the ball. Despite his penchant for cracking the whip and being hard on his players, Wade loved how fluid his team looked in the open floor this early.

"We had kids that could rebound, that could shoot, that could play defense, and Muggsy was the answer to all of our problems that we had the year before, in terms of guys playing the point guard position who weren't really point guards," said Wade. "My challenge was to keep all the egos in check. We had kids who were coming from these rival rec programs, and my job was to make them into an unselfish, cohesive group."

Also on the Dunbar roster were Karl and Keith Wallace, the buddies of David Wingate, who initially encouraged him to give basketball a try. Both guards were in their senior seasons, though Keith, who stood 6 foot 1, was a year older. He'd repeated a grade in junior high school and possessed a comedic talent that kept folks doubled over in laughter. Karl, 5 foot 10, was another funny character who, though not especially skilled, was a bench leader who yelled out the defenses and screens employed by the opposition. The youngest two of eleven kids, their older brothers Steve and Dwayne were accomplished former Poets who had gone on to play their college ball at the University of Missouri and the University of Pittsburgh, respectively.

Eric Green, a hard-nosed, aggressive 6-foot-3 defender who loved to knock heads in practice, was another athlete who would be among the team's role players. He was the star quarterback and an excellent defensive back on Dunbar's football team, as well as a standout baseball player attracting some attention from pro scouts. Tim Dawson's older brother Ellis, along with Kevin Amos and Priestly Reeves, rounded out the reserve unit.

Getting the team to overcome their petty rivalries was no simple matter for Wade. Confrontations, in the heat of those first battles, were unavoidable.

"Those first couple of practices, we were really going at it," said Keith Wallace. "Guys were fighting for positions. The returning players were trying to let the new guys know that we weren't giving up our minutes without a battle. There were no easy shots, no layups, things got really physical and intense. Everybody got along, but we were so competitive that on a few occasions, pushing and shoving gave way to some scuffles."

When punches were thrown, Coach Wade would yank the combatants out of practice and send them out of the gym to calm down, yelling, "We are a family! And family does not fight family!" After a few minutes, he'd summon those players back to practice. But there was a price to be paid. Wade would keep those guys after practice and say, "You guys interrupted my practice, so now you know what to do. Go get your bricks and get on the baseline because ya'll have some extra running to do."

"And he would wear us out," said Wallace. "And as you were doing that extra running, after already being exhausted after a four-hour practice, you were looking at the guy next to you, struggling through the same torture, and that bonded us even more."

It was soon apparent what the team's pecking order would be. David Wingate and Reggie Williams would be returning to their starting forward positions. Shooting guard Gary Graham was another returning starter whose place was secure. With the muscular newcomer Tim Dawson using his power and leaping ability to grab every rebound in sight, he would man the starting center position. And everyone knew that no one was challenging Muggsy for the starting point guard spot. The recent transfer Reggie Lewis, who could be used at both forward positions, as well as at guard and center, and OJ, who could play both the point and off-guard positions, plus the versatile sophomore Keith James, would be among the first players off the bench.

If anyone had the right to be upset with Muggsy's arrival, it should have been OJ. Had Muggsy not transferred to Dunbar, OJ would have been the team's starting floor general. Back when they were kids playing at the recreation center, OJ was actually considered the better player. For their entire young lives, Muggsy was the point guard while OJ, whose scoring ability at such a young age placed him among the top twelve-year-olds in the country, was the shooting guard. By the time they arrived in high school, OJ was considered more of a combination guard, a scorer who could also play the point. Though still a magnificent player, he knew that his friend had surpassed him in talent. OJ was only 5 foot 6 but could attack the rim, hit jump shots all over the floor, and score against anyone. He could easily slam the ball and, had he been at any other school, would have been the center of attention. He was a lock to be one of the first players off the bench and the leader of the second-string unit. But some players, especially those who were considered to be so good at such an early age, might not have been able to handle not starting. OJ could.

"Muggs and I, along with Jerry White and Reggie Williams, had been friends for as long as we could remember," said Wood. "Of course, I wanted to start, but I knew that Muggs was the better point guard when we got to high school. I tried my best to push him in practice and never conceded an inch. But Muggsy and I were like family, and we were all about winning."

Despite the fact that Wade had coached Muggsy's older

brother and had known him since he was a child, there was now a feeling-out process between them during the first few weeks of practice. The nature of their relationship had changed. Muggsy was unequivocal in his understanding that Wade was a great coach, but despite the respect he had for him and how he couldn't wait to play at Dunbar, some of the coach's tactics were difficult for him to comprehend. When he had learned to play the game at the Lafayette Recreation Center, he'd trained and practiced drills that were all related to basketball. Running around with sandbags on his back while carrying bricks seemed ludicrous to him. Bogues would roll his eyes before the start of practice and whisper toward his friend Reggie Williams, "Why are we practicing with these props? This man is crazy. What the hell do bricks have to do with playing basketball?"

But after a few weeks, Muggsy understood that he'd never been challenged like this before, and he started to enjoy the sense of accomplishment he had at the completion of those brutal practices. Instead of loathing them, he began to embrace them. He started walking into the gym after study hall, saying, "Where them bricks at?"

Wade had been thinking about ways to improve his team's strength and stamina, especially in the fourth quarter, when he came up with the brainstorm of training and practicing with bricks. A lot of homes in the neighborhood were being torn down, and the school lacked the luxury of a fancy weight room. One day in the late '70s, Wade grabbed one of the team managers and drove past some of the demolition sites in the neighborhood. They piled a supply of bricks in his car, took them back to the school, cut up some old baseball uniforms that the school didn't use anymore, wrapped them around the bricks, and then put duct tape around them.

In addition to strengthening their hands and arms, the bricks would give the team stamina to be fresh late in games. Wade intended his practices to teach the Poets the psychological advantage of being able to block out how tired they were or whatever pain they felt.

"My philosophy was to have a team that ran with the ball at every opportunity and that applied some serious defensive pressure," said Wade. "So in order to be able to do that full speed, for an entire game, especially in the fourth quarter when your arms would be tired, I thought the bricks would help us meet our objectives of being in the best condition possible."

While he felt that this team would be an offensive force with Muggsy pushing a frenetic fast break, Wade knew that if he could mold this group into a unit that took a collective pride in defensive excellence, he would have something truly special on his hands. As it turned out, Muggsy, almost singlehandedly, ensured that they would play with hunger and passion, because every time he stepped onto the court, he played as if he were trying to prove wrong every naysayer who had ever doubted him.

"From that very first practice, Muggsy owned the gym," said Darryl Wood. "It was like his focus was on an entirely different level. He played with such a hunger and competitiveness, and I guess he wanted to let everybody know, 'Hey, I'm here!'"

"It was fascinating to see how Coach Wade harnessed Muggsy's talent," said Eric Green. "They were both perfectionists. Coach pushed him hard, and Muggs loved being challenged like that. He was the perfect point guard for Coach's system. I knew I was probably going to be like the tenth guy off the bench, but I couldn't complain. As much of a competitor as I was, I realized how remarkable the guys ahead of me were. The things they were doing in practice were amazing."

"When I saw how Muggsy attacked everything during the first few practices, I knew that we were going to be really good. I mean, really, really good!" said Wade. "He was always very competitive, but there was something else going on."

What was going on was that Bogues realized that this was what he'd been dreaming about for as long as he could remember playing basketball. Watching the older legendary Poets like Skip Wise, Ernie Graham, and Dwayne Wood and experiencing the energy in the gym during Dunbar's games, he was now ready for his turn on the stage.

For the players who had never been a teammate of Muggsy's before, one of the first things they learned in those early practices was that if you didn't keep one eye on him whenever he had the ball, you ran the risk of getting smacked in the face with one of his bullet passes. He was throwing passes that they'd never seen before, coming from different angles and at speeds that they didn't know existed.

It didn't take long for Bogues's style of play to permeate the team. His intensity, hunger, and unselfishness became contagious. But the most glaring effect was on each practice's defensive intensity. At an early age, he learned that to be effective, he needed to use his size disadvantage to his own benefit. As great a ball handler and passer as he was, his biggest strength was his smothering defensive pressure. In practice, Wade drilled his team to execute a full-court press after every made free throw. They practiced it over and over. But even when they sat back in a man-to-man or zone defense, Bogues pressured the opposing point guard from baseline to baseline. With his speed, strength, low center of gravity, and fast hands, he would make an inordinate amount of steals and force his opponent to commit a traveling violation or make ill-advised passes in the face of pressure.

David Wingate and Gary Graham were already considered elite defenders, and Reggie Williams was very good as well. They took great pride in not allowing the man whom they were guarding to score. With Muggsy negating the effectiveness of the opposing team's point guard, the Poets became even more dangerous as a unit. Bogues generated in his teammates, already very prideful and skilled on the defensive end, a desire to dig deeper to live up to his standard. In addition, the rest of the team realized that if they didn't perform at a high level on the defensive end, they might not see the court during actual games.

"We called it 'getting in a guy's jock,' and no one in the world was as good as getting in a guy's jock as Muggsy," said the backup point guard Darryl "OJ" Wood. "We had always played together on the same teams growing up together in Lafayette. I would watch him stealing the ball all the time from everybody, but I never truly understood the fear that he instilled or the impact of his determination and intensity as a defender. He was a killer."

Despite being best friends, Bogues was annihilating OJ in those early practices, showing no mercy. OJ quickly realized that he had to fight back, so he tried to get up in Muggsy's jock just as hard. Everybody on the team had an ego and felt that if Muggsy could dominate a game with defense, then so could they.

"Coach Wade's coaching and teaching style was very much like he was parenting," said starting shooting guard Gary Graham. "It was like he was setting our goals so high for us because he was not going to be satisfied if we underachieved. When you wore that uniform, the expectation of excellence was already built in because Dunbar was a powerhouse. I grew up in that gym watching my older brother Ernie wear that uniform. It was electric. Everybody wanted to be a part of that. That was a very big responsibility that we all took seriously."

Graham's brothers had taught him that defense won games. They taught him that if he scored 20 points and the man whom he was guarding scored 20 as well, then he hadn't done anything. At a young age, his brothers taught him that not everybody could be the main scorer, but everybody could play great defense. In those first few weeks of practice, the team saw how devastating they were off steals and how much offense they would be able to generate through their defense because of Muggsy's mastery of running the fast break.

"We saw that by getting steals and creating turnovers, we could be unstoppable," said Graham. "And Mr. Wade was a tough defensive coach. That was going to be our calling card. He wouldn't get mad if you missed a shot. But if you didn't give your full effort on defense, he'd get pissed."

"The system that Coach Wade taught was perfect for me," said Bogues. "Playing at such a fast pace with constant pressure, and having those guys with me who could run, pass, shoot, and sky through the air, even though the practices could be brutal, they were so much fun."

With Graham's skills complementing Muggsy's, they were quite possibly the country's most suffocating defensive backcourt. Graham insisted on guarding the other team's best scorer, and he took great pride in shutting him down. Muggsy made the opponent's best ball handler fight and struggle for every inch on the court, making him worry about getting the ball stolen at any time. Graham was a big, strong, aggressive guard who had quick feet and always managed to keep his man in front of him. Muggsy learned to anticipate when Graham would force the man he was guarding to change direction off the dribble, and the diminutive guard would be right there to swipe the ball away.

The players were feeding off one another in other ways during those early practices as well. Tim Dawson would be forcefully blocking shots in practice, and the other guys would get hungry to block shots, too. When Reggie Williams soared through the air for a highlight reel dunk, Wingate, Reggie Lewis, and Dawson would try to rip the rims down when they got a chance to throw down an electrifying dunk. Nobody was complaining about how many shots or points they were getting in the early scrimmages.

"We could all sense this incredible feeling that we were connected, that what we were doing was really special because we were executing at such a high level," said Bogues.

One thing that all great teams have in common is synergy, a sense of purpose that every player buys into. Wade noticed that getting his team to buy into that sense of purpose was eased by the fact that they had known one another for a very long time. It went beyond a sense of familiarity and into the realm of family.

"We weren't just carrying the banner for ourselves," said Graham. "Dunbar was our family. There was a tradition, and we believed that we were supposed to win. That was the expectation. Those lofty goals were built in. When you stepped on the court with that maroon and gold on, it was showtime for the entire East Baltimore community. Those first few weeks of practice were so incredible because we were so strong at every position. We had guys on the second team and third team that were stars in their own right. Mr. Wade was like our dad and we were like fifteen of his sons."

After a few weeks, the Poets couldn't wait to test themselves against other teams. Their practices were becoming increasingly brutal. In the locker room after one practice, an exhausted Gary Graham announced, "Man, if this is how we're going against one another, imagine when we go against guys that we don't like!"

"Here Come the Show!"

AS THE TEAM WRAPPED up its preparation on December 2, the day before their first game—against Edmondson High School—Wade was anxious to see how they would perform in a game situation. His boys had beaten up one another in practice and showed him that they could be a dominant team. He knew that this was the best team that he had ever coached, that the Dunbar fans and the East Baltimore community were in for a special treat when they came out to watch them.

On the eve of the season, he knew that he'd drilled the team well, that they were frothing at the mouth to compete in a real game. But he still worried as he drove home the night before Dunbar's first game. He wondered how the boys would respond under the whistle in front of the big crowds. He couldn't help but flash back to the last game against Calvert Hall and speculate about what would happen when they were tested, how they would execute under pressure.

On Thursday afternoon, December 3, after classes dismissed, the Dunbar Poets scattered in various directions before making their way back to the gymnasium, where they were scheduled to assemble at 5:00 p.m. Some went home to change clothes and grab a quick bite to eat, while others went to the nearby Popeye's, McDonald's, or over to the Old Town Mall for an early dinner. They trickled back into the school and sat in the gym's bleachers, waiting for the team manager to walk out of Coach Wade's office and tell them that it was time to board the waiting bus.

The ride to their first away game was a short one, a little more than two miles through the city streets for their evening game against Edmondson in the opening contest of the Poet-Laker Invitational Tournament, which was being hosted by their rival Lake Clifton. Theirs was the featured game on the first night of the tournament, the opening day of Baltimore City's much anticipated high school basketball season. The players' excitement was difficult to contain. The young men were anxious to get their season under way, even a little nervous.

Once the players boarded the bus, they sat quietly, waiting for Wade. After locking his office and taking one last walk through the locker room, the coach sat down next to Lynn Badham, his assistant coach, and told the bus driver, "Let's go." Badham was a devout Christian from North Carolina with a thick Southern drawl who never cursed. The Poets would laugh when, frustrated or angry at practice, the normally calm and reserved assistant coach would yell out his signature phrase: "Dangblammit!!!"

During the brief ride, the players adhered to the coach's rules of traveling to an away game. There was no loud talking or clowning around. They were expected to be focused on the game.

"Coach Wade wanted everybody to be concentrating on the upcoming game during any bus ride," said Bogues. "We were respectful, but we were still sitting in the back cracking jokes. We all had a little bit of nerves, but we were still loose."

As they entered the packed Lake Clifton gymnasium, all eyes were on them. "Here come the show!" people shouted as the boys entered the gym. The boys sat together in the bleachers.

"We were the featured game that night, and it seemed like the whole city of Baltimore came out to see us play," said Wade. "Everybody knew that we had Wingate, Reggie Williams, and Gary Graham coming back. And the buzz about Muggsy was unreal. They came out that night to see what all the fuss was about."

As they waited for the previous game to reach the end of the third quarter, the boys sat, looking serious, seemingly in their own bubble. Although the gym was filled with friends, family members, and schoolmates, the Poets kept to themselves. Whenever they traveled to an away game, even if it was right down the street at Lake Clifton, they knew that it was a business trip. Another of Wade's many rules was that they were not allowed to speak to their friends or family or anybody else before the game. If one of them had to go to the bathroom, they went together. It was understood that they weren't there for a social event.

As the buzzer sounded for the end of the third quarter, the boys walked downstairs to their locker room. As they sauntered in, Muggsy saw his uniform, folded neatly on the bench, with his Nike sneakers and fresh new socks laid out on the floor underneath. He slid into his shorts and stared at his Dunbar jersey, hardly believing that this moment had finally arrived.

"The butterflies were intense; I was nervous," said Bogues. "I had dreamed about this moment ever since I was a little kid. And it was like all those questions about could I really play high school ball, all the voices of people who said I was too small, all of that was going through my mind. I was a little emotional, too, because I was looking around the locker room at OJ, Jerry White, and Reggie, the guys who I used to play with."

Bogues looked at Wingate and Lewis and recalled the great rec league battles that he'd had with them. He thought about his sister, Sherron, who was in the gym, waiting for him to make his Dunbar debut. He reflected on his father, now in prison at Jessup, wishing he could be there to witness his special moment. And he was also slightly disappointed that his mother didn't understand the significance of him being the starting point guard at Dunbar.

"My mom wasn't into basketball; she didn't know how good I really was yet," said Bogues. "I was ready to get out there and show everybody that I was a player. It was such an emotional night for me. And I loved putting on that uniform. I felt so proud, looking at the word *POETS* on the front, the maroon with gold-and-white trim and the zigzag design on the side."

Wade stood in front of a chalkboard and, after letting Coach Badham say a few words to the team, issued a challenge to all of his starters. "Russ, I want at least eighteen points and ten rebounds," he said. "Same for you, David, along with two steals. Gary, I need you to take two charges, give us at least fifteen points, and get three steals. Timmy, I want at least ten points and ten rebounds and four blocked shots. And I want you to catch Muggsy's passes!"

Everybody laughed because of the starting five, Tim Dawson was having the most trouble corralling the improbable passes that the little point guard was sending his way. "And Muggsy," Wade continued, "I want you to push it, honey! Run the show and give us at least ten assists. Our defense will create our offense, so let's get after it and run up and down and play our game. We've spent enough time beating up on one another. Let's go beat up on somebody else."

The boys formed a circle, put their hands together, and started chanting, "Poets Gettin' Ready to Roll!" over and over. Each time they repeated it, their voices grew louder and louder, until the muffled sound of their shouts could be heard throughout the hallway and stairwell leading up to the gym. They walked up the stairs, looking regal in their maroon warm-up suits. At the front of the line stood Wade's six-year-old son, Darion, wearing his own maroon-and-gold outfit. With Darion leading the charge, the boys burst into the gym to a cacophony of roars. Lined up in size order, Muggsy led the team for a jog around the gym and to the half-court line, where they separated into three staggered lines of five players each, the two guards in front and the three big men slightly behind. Bogues slammed the ball against the hardwood, initiating a mesmerizing warm-up routine that began with a five-man weave.

"We drilled everything in practice, over and over, until it was perfected, including the warm-up routine," said Wade.

After each unit completed a few dizzying five-man weaves, where the ball zipped in and out of their hands with uncanny precision as players sped toward the rim, the next unit executed the drill, followed by the next. After a few rotations, they formed a single-file line, again in size order, following behind Muggsy as he dribbled up the court and gently laid the ball off the backboard. Running behind him, OJ flew through the air, caught the ball with two hands above the rim, and tapped it back off the backboard. Each following player did the same, until Reggie Williams caught the final tap and, with his forearm way above the rim, gently dropped the ball through the net. As they dispersed to the separate corners of the half-court, they began a meticulous four-corner passing drill as a blur of whizzing balls and streaking players flew around with military precision.

As many maroon-clad fans in the crowd stomped and began yelling, "POET PRIDE! POET PRIDE!" the dancing cheerleaders on the baseline broke into their pregame cheer:

Poets!
It's so hard, it's so hard to be a Poet!
It's so hard!
Go Fight Win!
Shake that thing!
Gimme a G, Gimme an O, Gimme an F, Gimme an I,
Gimme a G, Gimme an H, Gimme a T,
Gimme a W, Gimme an I, Gimme an N!
What's it spell? Go Fight Win!
Shake that thing!

When Dunbar won the opening tip and the ball was placed in Muggsy's hand, the speed with which he attacked the Edmondson defense drew gasps from the crowd.

Dribble, Dribble
Shoot, Shoot
Take that ball to the hoop hoop hoop!
Dribble, Dribble
Shoot, Shoot
Take that ball to the hoop hoop hoop!

As the cheerleaders danced and yelled, Bogues and the Dunbar Poets were off and running. Sherron Bogues might have been, barring little kids, one of the smallest people in the crowd, but her ear-piercing screams could be heard by everyone as she repeatedly screamed, "Go Shorty! Yeah! Go Shorty! Yeah! Go

Shorty! Go Shorty! Go Shorty!" exhorting her little brother to play the game she had first shown him when he watched her playing against the neighborhood boys.

"As soon as that ball tipped off, all of the nervousness and apprehension went right out of the window," said Bogues. "I was right back in my comfort zone, on the court with the ball in my hands, running with my boys. And for anybody that thought I wouldn't be able to handle the high school game, they shut up very quickly. Not only was I on a mission that night, but the whole team was on a mission. And that was the first time that I truly experienced what a crowd could do for a basketball team. Our rec league games were always crowded, but it wasn't anything like that energy that I felt during that first Dunbar game."

Unfortunately for Edmondson, they felt the consequences of Bogues's energy, too. David Wingate led all scorers with 23 points and Dunbar's new center, Tim Dawson, controlled the boards with his 13 rebounds and 19 points, many of which came off offensive rebounds. But no other player made quite as big an impression as the team's point guard.

"I'd heard so much about Muggsy before he came to Dunbar, but I never saw him play rec league ball," said Assistant Coach Badham. "I kept hearing about this little point guard that was so good, that the first time I saw him, I said, 'Wow! That guy is so tiny. How in the world can he be that good?' When I saw the things he was doing in practice, I said, 'Wow! This little guy is amazing.' But there was nothing that could prepare you, even after having watched him in practice for three weeks, for seeing him play in a real game."

After the opening tip against Edmondson, Badham had to control himself from jumping off the bench every time Muggsy stole the ball or dribbled through double and triple teams and left defenses behind as though nobody were there. He threw alley-oop passes to David Wingate or Reggie Williams that they slammed through the rim.

"I couldn't take my eyes off him," said Badham. "He was hyp-notizing."

Dunbar destroyed Edmondson, which was considered a very good team, 90–36. And despite the unit's polish and convincing performance, and the great play of the seniors Wingate and Graham, along with the juniors Williams and Dawson, the revelation was Tyrone "Muggsy" Bogues, who had 15 steals, 12 assists, and 4 points.

"People had never seen anything like Muggsy before, and it was hard for some to comprehend that he could be the most valuable player on the team without scoring a point," said Wade. "He controlled the game on defense because Edmondson's point guard could hardly get the ball across half-court. He would drop into the paint without being seen, and as soon as the opposing forwards or center tried to make a dribble move, he was right there to swipe the ball."

With Bogues pushing the pace, the Dunbar fast break was unstoppable. He spread the ball around to everybody. The Poets were flying downcourt and dunking the ball mercilessly against Edmondson.

"Timmy Dawson was blocking shots, and David and Reggie and Gary were hitting deep and midrange shots," said Wade. "It was really an excellent performance."

But their amazing play and intensity did not stop Wade from riding them mercilessly, picking out a weakness that each player had, no matter how miniscule, and making it seem like it was a major flaw in their game. No matter how good they were, he wanted to let them know that they still had weaknesses, that there was always room for them to improve.

One player that Wade was particularly intrigued with was the sinewy junior newcomer whom everybody called Truck, Reggie Lewis. Lewis looked almost frail, and Wade worried whether he would be able to handle the physical battles. But after the first set of practices, those worries proved unwarranted. Lewis had yet to play high school ball. As a second-string center and forward, he was matched up in rebounding drills, half-court sets, and full-court scrimmages with Dawson, the tough banger in the paint who could jump up and down like a jackrabbit, and with David Wingate and Reggie Williams, who were at the top of every college recruiter's prospect list. Lewis proved to be a scrappy, willing adversary.

"Truck was so laid-back, I thought he might get pushed around," said Wade. "He'd played well in the rec leagues, but this was going to be his first year of high school ball. He was very raw and still learning the game, but his potential really excited me."

Wade thought about starting him, because he felt that Lewis gave the team a better offensive punch than Dawson did. He was impressed with his soft hands, whereas Dawson had problems handling some of Muggsy's passes.

"Truck could do things in the paint with his back to the basket and on the perimeter," said Wade. "He could score in unorthodox ways. He wasn't flamboyant, but he was effective."

Lewis's game was very much like his personality. He was quiet but much tougher than Wade thought he would be. The coach decided to play him off the bench because Dawson was such a strong rebounder and shot blocker that he would set that tone for the Poets with the starting unit. But when Reggie Lewis came in off the bench, Wade felt that they would be a better offensive team.

Wade was perplexed by Reggie Lewis's personality, though. He thought that by being abrasive and challenging him, he could help the quiet, socially tentative newcomer come out of his shell. But he would come to find out that Lewis was not being quiet because he was new to the team and trying to get his bearings; he was simply naturally shy and introverted. Due to his unassuming nature, Lewis was often underestimated. His story, like those of many of his peers, was already characterized by his overcoming daunting obstacles at that point in his life and having an inner strength of character that kept propelling him forward.

———

Lewis's father, Irvin Lewis Sr., was known as Butch to his family, friends, and others in the East Baltimore community where the family lived. Butch walked the city streets selling fruit from a horse-drawn buggy, known in the local vernacular as an "Arab-er." He'd also buy and sell worn appliances and furniture, bringing home some of the nicer items to furnish the family's rented row houses. Reggie's mother, Inez, more commonly known by her nickname Peggy, raised her four children as well as her youngest sister on not much more than love.

The family subsisted on food stamps and welfare checks because Peggy, despite being so young, had already suffered a heart attack when she was just seventeen years old. She'd been diagnosed as having a heart murmur and leaky valves. There was a history of heart problems in Peggy's family. Her youngest son, Jon, was born with a small hole in his heart, which required surgery when he was just four years old. By the time Reggie was six years old, the family had already lived in six different row houses. But because all of the homes were located in the same neighborhood, Reggie and his siblings never had to change schools or become acclimated to new environments and different friends.

Despite being so skinny, Lewis had an unbelievable appetite.

When he was five years old, he acquired the nickname that would stay with him for the remainder of his life. After watching him devour a number of dinners and then eat leftovers off other people's plates one night, a family member said that he resembled a walking garbage truck. From that day on, his family and soon the entire neighborhood began calling him Truck. As a kid, he preferred playing football and baseball. But as his older brother Irvin became interested in basketball, Reggie followed behind him. The two would hit the Collington Square basketball courts in East Baltimore, sometimes after midnight, when the suffocating Maryland humidity and summer heat had cooled, to practice their skills and play one-on-one.

In middle school, Reggie already stood 6 foot 4. His sister's boyfriend would work on defense and ball-handling drills with him and take him to different parts of the city to play against people he didn't know so that he could challenge himself. In the same way that Muggsy and Reggie Williams were nurtured by Leon Howard at the Lafayette Recreation Center, David Wingate, Gary Graham, and Reggie Lewis were mentored by Anthony "Dudie" Lewis at the Cecil Kirk Recreation Center. In the late '70s, Dudie was coaching Irvin Lewis at Cecil Kirk. Irvin was a very good player, and Dudie often heard him talking about his little brother Reggie.

"Reggie was about twelve years old when he first started coming around to Cecil Kirk," said Anthony Lewis. "Irvin used to talk about this little brother he had. Except when we met Reggie, we saw that he was five inches taller than Irvin was. We said, 'Damn, we gotta get this kid in the program.' Reggie started developing an affection for basketball. At that early age, he had some physical attributes, some length and some size. He also had an enormous work ethic to go along with a sweet smile."

Reggie spent his first year of high school at Patterson, where

Irvin was the star on the basketball team. His dream was to play on the same high school team with his brother. He was devastated when the Patterson coach cut him. Anthony Lewis was amazed that the Patterson coach could not see the potential that Reggie possessed. Dudie believed that the best option for Reggie was to transfer to Dunbar to play his two remaining years of high school ball. Dudie had had success with some of his mentees who'd spent time at other high schools before transferring to Dunbar, like Ernie Graham, Gary Graham's older brother, who came in from Lake Clifton, and David Wingate, who spent his first year at Northern High School. He saw that Wade was a disciplinarian who made his players better, not only in basketball, but as students and young men.

"I thought that playing for Bob Wade at Dunbar provided the best opportunities that these kids could have on the high school level," said Anthony Lewis. "I wanted my kids to be coached, to have structure and a chance to advance to as high a level as was possible for them. It wasn't like I was telling my kids, 'Hey, leave that school.' When they came to me and said that they wanted to be someplace else, I'd ask them to describe what they wanted the new place to be like. For some kids, Dunbar wasn't a good fit. But for guys like Wingate and Reggie, I knew it would be, because they were the type of players who could take Wade being so tough on them. They would run through a wall if you told them that was how they were going to get better."

When Dudie told Wade that Reggie would be coming to Dunbar for his eleventh-grade year, the coach listened but didn't have a true frame of reference for this new player. He trusted Dudie's word but had some lingering doubts, considering that Reggie hadn't made the team at Patterson High School. Wade watched him play for Cecil Kirk over the summer before his junior year.

After seeing him not merely holding his own, but excelling while competing against other talented recreation center teams, Wade approached Anthony Lewis and said, "That damn coach at Patterson must be crazy to cut this kid."

But as much as Wade was enthralled with Reggie Lewis's potential, that did not stop him from the occasional verbal barrage that every Dunbar player experienced. When Lewis had his first talk with Wade at the beginning of the school year, like all of the team's newcomers, he was told that he would be required to practice with the cross country team to improve his conditioning and would be required to attend mandatory study halls.

"I told Reggie and the rest of the new guys that they had to abide by the Wade Rules," said Wade. "That meant that they were required to go to class, put their best foot forward academically, turn in all their assignments on time, be at practice on time, be prepared to work harder in the classroom and on the basketball court than they'd ever worked before, and that in everything they do, they accept responsibility and never make excuses."

Reggie Lewis, like Muggsy, was a newcomer who was more than ready for this season to begin. He was ready to prove that he was one of the best players in the city. But he was not prepared for Wade's in-your-face motivational tactics and coaching style. At the outset, Wade started harping on his conditioning and speed. The coach might have been tough on Lewis, but he liked what he saw out of the kid.

"Reggie was consistent and reliable in the sense that whatever I told him that he wasn't good at, he was determined to prove me wrong," said Wade. "And I loved how he retained information, how I didn't have to go over things repeatedly with him. He was eager to learn and would do more than what was asked of him."

But Reggie was having some difficulty in getting acclimated to the new team. The other players liked him, and he had a kindred spirit in star player Reggie Williams, because they were both so quiet and reserved. But he loathed being screamed at during practices. And he was unhappy that he would be playing the center and forward positions most of the time, as he envisioned himself as more of a perimeter player.

"I was shocked by how quiet Truck was," said Williams. "I hardly ever talked, but he talked even less than I did. We called him Cookie Monster because he loved chocolate chip cookies. And he always had some cookies on him, in his pockets or in his book bag. One time after practice, I was hungry and asked him for some cookies. And he looked at me and said no. I said, 'Man you gonna give me two or three of them cookies!' And he just laughed and gave me some."

"Truck came to talk to me, and it was a difficult adjustment for him during those first few weeks of practice," said Cecil Kirk's Lewis. "That was a major test of his maturation. He didn't like the fact that he was playing center and that he wasn't starting. But I told him that he had to understand that at six foot seven, playing in the post was going to be what was best for the team."

Anthony Lewis stressed that by practicing every day against players like Reggie Williams, Tim Dawson, and David Wingate, all of whom were being recruited by major colleges, Truck was going to have a great opportunity to improve and expand his skill set. He told his protégé that he would still be able to showcase some of the things that he could do on the perimeter even while playing center, and how the next two years of preparation would be of great benefit once he transitioned to playing full-time as a guard on the college level.

"I just told him to have trust in what Wade was doing," said

Lewis. "But I never had to tell him to keep working hard because whenever he stepped on the court, scrapping and giving his full effort was part of who he naturally was."

———

Although a few national publications were touting Calvert Hall as the nation's top team heading into the season, a rival coach intimately familiar with both Dunbar and Calvert Hall politely disagreed. "I think the wrong team is rated number one in the country," the coach at Lake Clifton, Woody Williams, told the *Baltimore Sun* in the winter of 1981. "The quality of Wade's team is one of the best-kept secrets in the country."

"With our starting five and the guys we had coming off the bench, there was no question in our mind that we were the best team in the country," said Reggie Williams. "We were hungry to show everybody else what we already knew."

The Poet-Laker Invitational was a three-day event, but the final two days of competition were held at Dunbar. So on the very next evening after their dominant win over Edmondson, the Poets were in their own gym to face another tough city team in Frederick Douglass High School. With 3:31 elapsed in the first quarter, the Poets were leading by 4 points. They proceeded to go on a 16–6 run that effectively removed any suspense about the game's outcome. Williams scored 25 points, Dawson scored 15, and Wingate and Graham added 12 apiece. The team's lone sophomore, the lanky, smooth-shooting Keith James, came off the bench to score 10. Bogues was, again, a force of nature with his collection of assists, steals, and overall floor generalship. Late in the third quarter, Wade substituted for his entire starting five while holding a decisive 27-point lead. With OJ handling the sec-ond-team point guard duties, and Reggie Lewis exhibiting the elite level of talent on Dunbar's bench, the reserves pushed the lead to 40.

"When Truck, OJ, Keith James, the Wallace brothers, and the rest of the reserves got their chance to get in the game, man, we were into it," said Bogues. "And they were just as hungry as we were, maybe even more. They wanted to show everybody that they were just as good as the starters. We were on the bench screaming and yelling while they ran the ball down Douglass's throat. And as a team, we didn't miss anything when they took the floor, because it was the same thing: steals, pretty passes, and a whole lot of dunks and easy buckets off our defensive pressure and the fast break. It was dunk city out there."

The team's second and third unit knew that expectations for them were the same as for the starting unit. As long as there was time on the clock, they were expected to play a certain style of aggressive basketball that characterized Dunbar's competitive philosophy. It didn't matter if they were first-string or third-string, they knew that if they didn't box out, if they didn't pass ahead to the open man, if they didn't play that "in your jock" defense and concentrate on shutting down the weak side baseline rebounding, they'd be right back on that bench sitting next to Coach Wade.

During the team's first two games against Edmondson and Frederick Douglass, the Poets were formidable. Although it was a small sample of work, Wade was pleased. The thought of how good they could be drove him to want to push them even harder. But that would have to wait, because in their third game in three nights, Dunbar would be facing a very tough opponent and one of their biggest rivals in the Lakers of Lake Clifton High School, one of the teams that had beaten them the season before.

In the Poet-Laker Invitational, Lake Clifton's Melvin Mathis had been impressive in his opening game performances. A 6-foot-8 power forward with size and width, Mathis weighed about 260 pounds and had already received scholarship offers from Villanova, Wake Forest, North Carolina State, Maryland, Georgia Tech, Clemson, Tulsa, Drake, Xavier, Northeastern, Iowa, and Connecticut, among others. He'd scored 32 and 25 points in the Lakers' first two victories and looked unstoppable. Wade felt that he had enough height to match up with Mathis, but his forwards were slim guys who could run fast; they weren't bulky bangers. Nevertheless, he was confident that Lake Clifton did not have the depth to run with his team for four quarters.

"Mathis has had a very good tournament and whoever is guarding him, just do your best and make him work for everything he gets," Wade told his team in the locker room prior to the championship game. "We are going to confuse them with all of the defenses we'll throw at them, and they're not going to be able to withstand our pressure."

Wade conceded to Assistant Coach Lynn Badham that Mathis might get his points, but he was confident that the Poets' pressure defense would contain the rest of the team.

The boys gathered in their pregame locker room huddle, put their hands together, and began their chant, "Poets Gettin' Ready to Roll! Poets Gettin' Ready to Roll!" Lake Clifton had beaten them twice during the prior season, and the Poets knew that this game was going to tell them a lot about where they stood at this early juncture of the 1981–1982 campaign.

At the end of the first quarter, Dunbar led by only one point, 15–14. Despite the close score, Bogues set the tone in the game's opening minutes, stripping Lakers' guard Tommy Foster three possessions in a row.

"Tommy was one of those guys who liked to talk a lot, and before the game started, he kept telling me how he was going to post me up," said Bogues. "He was laughing and smiling and sounded like he was really confident before tip-off. He was talking a lot of trash, talking about what he was gonna do and how, as he said, he was 'gonna back the little fella into the post.' But once that whistle blew, I took him out of his game. He liked to bring the ball up the court with a high dribble, and that was a no-no against me."

After Lake Clifton's Carl Fair scored on a thunderous dunk in the second quarter, in which the crowd started yelling that it looked like he'd jumped from the top of the bleachers, Wade angrily called for a time-out and inserted Reggie Lewis. The Poets then proceeded to outscore the Lakers 21–7 and took a 15-point lead at halftime.

In the third quarter alone, Gary Graham scored 9 points, while Reggie Williams chipped in with 8, including a spectacular two-handed dunk that shook the gym. With Williams and Wingate taking turns guarding Mathis, and Wade's masterful defensive play calling as the Poets alternated between a suffocating man-to-man and a 1–2–2 zone, Lake Clifton's star was visibly frustrated with Dunbar's length and speed.

"A lot of people were giving me credit for shutting down Mathis," said Wingate. "But it really was a team effort. Tim [Dawson] and Russ [Reggie Williams] took turns guarding him, too. But the guys who deserved the most credit for how we held him in check were Muggs and Gary. Muggs was so effective as a one-man pressing machine, and he was ripping the ball from their guards so much. Gary, like he always did, shut his man down."

By the time the Lake Clifton guards were able to get the ball over half-court, if Muggsy hadn't already stolen the ball, their offense was invariably out of sync. With his frustration boiling over, Mathis, having scored an inconsequential 8 points, was ejected from the game in the fourth quarter, along with Gary Graham, following a heated shouting and shoving match. Things got tense for a minute, as Graham's older brothers came out of the stands and onto the court, ready to fight. But once both players were ejected, things simmered down.

"Gary and Melvin had an intense rivalry that had been going back years," said Wade. "They competed against each other growing up on the playgrounds and in the rec centers. Melvin played for the Madison Square Rec Center and Gary was a product of Cecil Kirk Rec, so that pushing and shoving and the way they were going at each other was really a neighborhood thing. Gary's family was very close, and to his older brothers, he was the baby and they were extremely overprotective of him."

Williams led all scorers with a dominating 31-point performance. Although he did not score a single point, Bogues provided the heavy foot on Dunbar's accelerator during the Poets' 76–45 victory. He continually sped downcourt, dribbling and weaving through the tight Laker defense, lofting demoralizing alley-oops to his teammates.

"The crowd was going berserk," said Bogues. "I threw alley-oops to Gate, Reg, and Timmy, and we were balling! I knew I didn't have to score. My job was to control the tempo and impact the game in other ways. We won by thirty-one! I knew what my guys could do, and I loved getting them the ball, orchestrating, setting them up for easy buckets. Scoring never mattered that much to me. I was having so much fun out there just dishing the ball and running the show, being a playmaker."

"They beat the crap out of us," said Carl Fair, Lake Clifton's starting center. "Muggsy was so good, it was frightening. Their defense was incredible. It totally disrupted our offense. And they were so quick and long. And even if you beat them and got to the rim, they had Tim Dawson in the paint, and he could jump to the moon and block everything. Reggie Williams and David Wingate were blocking shots left and right, too. And it seemed like Gary Graham didn't miss—he just shot the lights out. And as quick as they got a rebound or steal, the ball would be in Muggsy's hands and that's when things got outrageous because he had all those guys on the wing that could finish above the rim. Muggsy was the best player I ever saw in transition and passing the ball, especially his alley-oops. He was like nitroglycerin because when the ball was in his hands, the alley-oops just exploded. And then you had Reggie Williams, who was the best player in the country. He had such a sweet jump shot, all these spin moves, and he could post up on the blocks and hit a jump hook with either hand. They were so good, it was scary."

With the championship in hand, Wade let his boys enjoy themselves for a few moments in the locker room. He also took a few moments to relax and soak it all in. But before dismissing his team, he wanted to make sure they understood that bigger tests lay ahead.

"Just because we won three games, that means nothing," Wade told his players, before sending them home. "When we step back on the court for practice on Monday, we are 0–0. To me, you haven't beaten anybody yet. You guys played pretty well, but you also made a lot of mistakes that I am not happy with. When we get back in the gym, we will correct them. And if you think we've worked hard up to this point, believe me, we haven't done anything yet."

Lake Clifton's coach Woody Williams said that Wade's team, from what he'd seen in the first three games, was already, in his opinion, one of the best teams in Dunbar's illustrious history. When a local reporter relayed that statement to Wade, he simply said, "Only time will tell how far this team can go. But they are a very cohesive group."

Wade wanted to keep his team hungry. There was only a handful of games in the upcoming days, against teams he felt they should handily defeat. But he knew that after feasting on some local prey, his Poets would be in for their first true test of the year. They would be heading on their first road trip of the season in the next few weeks, to New York City, to compete in the Harlem Holiday Classic, where they would get to test their mettle against some of the top teams the Big Apple had to offer.

CHAPTER FIVE

"You Want to Sit Down and Cry, It Makes You So Sad"

AFTER WINNING THE POET-LAKER Invitational Championship, Muggsy stopped in to see his mentor, Leon Howard, at the Lafayette Recreation Center. Howard was excited about his young protégé's progress, especially after the previous year's difficulties while Muggsy was stuck at Southern. The rec center was Muggsy's second home. Growing up, he and his friends spent the majority of their time there, soaking up Mr. Howard's stories about his own college playing days, along with the ones he told about the great players from Lafayette who came before them.

Leon Howard was much more than a man who ran the local recreation center. His mentorship and tutelage of the players from the Lafayette Courts housing projects brought Baltimore recognition as an incubator of some of the country's top athletic talent. It wasn't always that way.

Howard had played his college ball at Johnson C. Smith College in Charlotte, North Carolina (now Johnson C. Smith University), a historically black school whose athletic teams competed in the CIAA, the Central Intercollegiate Athletic Association. One of his former teammates from Greensboro, North Carolina, was named Fred Neal. Neal would eventually become known worldwide by his nickname, Curly, when he replaced the legendary Marques Haynes as the premier ball handler on the Harlem Globetrotters from 1963 to 1985.

"The style that we played in college was way ahead of its time," said Howard. "Watch the highlights that they show on ESPN today, and that's the same game that we were playing, away from the national spotlight, back in the early 1960s! They tried to say we couldn't play, made derogatory statements that we played like racehorses, but if you watch LeBron James and Kevin Durant in the NBA today, or some of the best college teams like Kentucky or North Carolina, they play the same exact fast-break style that we were playing back then."

In the 1930s, a young University of Kansas undergraduate, an excellent all-around athlete who was part Delaware Indian and part African American named John McLendon, was studying under Dr. James Naismith, who invented the game of basketball while working as an instructor at the International Training School of the Young Men's Christian Association in Springfield, Massachusetts, in 1891. Naismith was Kansas's athletic director when McLendon came under his tutelage.

McLendon graduated from Kansas and became a successful high school coach. His first college head coaching job came at the North Carolina College for Negroes, a CIAA school in Durham that is now known as North Carolina Central University, where he coached from 1941 to 1952 and dominated, winning the CIAA conference crown seven times. He also coached at another CIAA institution, Hampton Institute, now known as Hampton University, and at Tennessee State A&I University, now known as Tennessee State, where his teams captured three straight NAIA titles. He was the first college coach, white or black, to win three consecutive national championships.

McLendon fielded teams that played at a frenetic offensive pace while incorporating an aggressive, full-court defense. He is widely regarded as the father of the fast break, employing a style that stressed pushing the ball on offense, shooting within eight seconds of taking possession, and rotating fresh players in and out of the game to tire out opponents while applying consistent pressure on both sides of the ball, from baseline to baseline. Those innovations spread through the other CIAA schools, such as Johnson C. Smith, where Leon Howard played. Other coaches had no choice but to keep pace with McLendon's teams or risk being run out of the gym. Unbeknownst even to him, Leon Howard walked into the Lafayette Recreation Center armed with a basketball blueprint passed along from the game's founder, Naismith, via his most innovative disciple, McLendon.

When Howard came to work as the director of the Lafayette Recreation Center in 1967, no one could have predicted how successfully he would realize the potential of young athletes growing up in the surrounding housing projects. But when he first stepped into the Lafayette Rec in late June of 1967, Howard was shocked. It was simply a large activity room with a Ping-Pong table that sat on the adjoining stage. There were two smaller connected rooms, one of which contained a set of weights. The other room was just big enough to house a pool table and nothing else. When he wanted to run an arts and crafts activity, Howard would simply throw a piece of plywood on top of the pool table. Most of the kids who came in were content to sit around playing checkers and cards. During the summer camp program, there would be at least a hundred kids jammed into the center for the full day, Monday through Friday.

Basketball, especially the professional game, was seen as a second-class pursuit at the time, despite the fact that all-time greats like Wilt Chamberlain, Oscar Robertson, Elgin Baylor, and Earl Monroe were elevating the game to levels that wouldn't be fully appreciated until a generation later. Howard was itching to teach the kids how to play basketball, but at the outset, he had to work within the confines of the center's physical limitations. But while he was coaching youth football and baseball teams, he was scouting, looking for players who possessed a natural athleticism and desire. When an organization called Operation Champ would block off streets in the neighborhood and set up portable basketball hoops on certain weekends, the kids, no matter how unskilled, flooded those makeshift courts. "I need to get me some basketball goals," he constantly said to himself.

In February of 1969, a fire in a West Baltimore church storage facility destroyed all of its contents, save for one portable basketball hoop. One of the staff members from Operation Champ informed Howard that he could have the hoop that survived the fire. An ecstatic Howard secured a truck from the housing department, picked up the portable goal, and set it up in the recreation center. Now he needed another hoop to hold full-court games.

Howard never simply threw the ball out on the court, letting the kids play around at their leisure. His intent was to teach them the science of the game. Unable to run an actual full-court game in the rec center, he insisted on doing drills that improved ball handling, defensive footwork, bounce passes, chest passes, strength, and conditioning.

"I taught them the fundamentals first and foremost," Howard said.

When—thanks to building custodians and cash from Howard's pocket—the second basket went up in the summer of 1969, the basketball program at Lafayette was off and running. One of the first things Howard did was start a league for kids in different age groups, an incubator where he could teach his neophytes the feel of real games.

"We'd practice every day, different teams from the different age groups had their own practice times, and we established something that no one else in the city had, and that was a house league," said Howard. "Those kids looked forward to playing in that house league."

The center did not own basketball uniforms. Instead, the kids used baseball and softball jerseys. At the conclusion of their game, each team was required to hand the jerseys they'd just played in to the next team for the ensuing contest. With the sweltering heat of the center, those shirts would be soaking wet after a couple of games. Poor apparel aside, though, the basketball house league at Lafayette instantly became the center's most popular activity.

"I was pretty lucky with that first group of twelve-year-olds that I had," said Howard. "I knew, by watching them play baseball and football, that they had potential as athletes. I just had to teach them the game. Those kids would prove to be my first powerhouse, the team that established Lafayette as a basketball force. They all came from the projects and were good friends."

He had no idea that he was teaching the core group that would put Baltimore basketball on the national map one day. He also got lucky in another equally important way, by forging a relationship with another local coach, basketball enthusiast, and ghetto celebrity, a mentor in the community since the 1950s named Edgar

Lee Bell. He was a slim man who stood only 5 foot 5. The neighborhood kids referred to him either as Mr. Lee or Tweety Bird.

"Mr. Lee had been living in that area for a ton of years; he knew all the kids who were good ballplayers going back many years before I got there," said Howard. "He not only knew all of the good players in the city, but he'd coached their fathers and uncles going back to when they were kids. He knew talent and was an excellent coach. He was very instrumental in Lafayette becoming a dominant force in the city."

Within a few short months, the Lafayette teams that walked into other centers in their softball jerseys went from being a laughingstock to a powerhouse. And Lafayette soon had its first star, a gangly kid named Allen Wise Jr., more popularly known by his nickname, Skip.

When Skip caught the basketball bug, watching Earl "the Pearl" Monroe and the Baltimore Bullets play at the downtown Civic Center, he began to live at the recreation center.

"When my mother took me to watch Earl Monroe play, that was something special," said Wise. "I never saw anybody do the things that he could do. When I saw how he electrified the crowd, the control he had over the ball and the fanciness of what he did on the court, it influenced me to want to play every day."

Howard, noting Skip's rapid development, took him to a tryout for Baltimore's Youth Games team when he was about twelve years old. The Youth Games were like a mini-Olympics, with each city sending its best young athletes to compete in various sports at competitions around the country. Wise was easily one of the most talented twelve-year-olds at the tryouts and made the team, but Howard would have to chase after him to get him to the team's practices. Howard understood the potential Wise possessed and what type of basketball player he could one day blossom into. And he was adamant that Wise travel outside of Baltimore to get a taste of national competition, hoping that it would motivate him to take the game seriously.

"Mr. Howard says that I got serious about basketball once I made the Youth Games, but that's not true," said Wise. "When I made the Youth Games roster, that's when *he* got serious about me! Sometimes, I didn't want to go to those practices; I wanted to play with my friends. I used to try to duck him, but he would run me down and drag me there."

When Skip wouldn't show up at the appointed time to go to practice, Howard would go all over the projects looking for him. And every time he found him, Skip would tell him the same thing. "I ain't going down there anymore, Mr. Howard, I don't want to play!"

"He'd tell me, 'Boy! You're going and that's it!'" said Wise. "And he would physically put me in his car. Mr. Howard was a strong man and there wasn't any use of me resisting. I'd be sitting in the backseat of his Pontiac GTO, huffing and puffing the whole ride. I would be so angry, but I would take that anger out on the basketball court, against all those other players. After a while, I began to understand that Mr. Howard had a plan for me. All those hours working on fundamentals and drills, learning plays and practicing all kinds of game situations, and then seeing how we went from a bunch of scrubs playing in softball jerseys to beating everybody in the city, it hit me that he not only had a plan for me, he had a plan for the whole team, the rec center, and the entire Lafayette Projects. That's when I started wanting to be good."

A happy-go-lucky kid who flashed a million-dollar smile most of the time, Wise became mean when the game began.

"It got to the point where Mr. Howard would have to put me out of the center," said Wise. "That place became my home. My mother would leave my food for me and go about her business because she wouldn't expect me to come home until it was late. When I started to feel like I was better than kids my age, I was no longer satisfied with just beating the guys I was coming up with. I wanted to beat everybody."

"That damn Skip would be talking trash during our one-on-one games and the same way I would call him names to get him upset, he started calling me Fat Man and Fat Howard," said Howard. "After that, all the kids that came into the center started calling me that. By the time Muggsy and Reggie Williams came along, playing to standing-room-only crowds and winning all those championships when they were ten years old, everybody all over the city knew me by that name."

Those one-on-one games, filled with trash talking, always unfolded in the same manner. Howard would shoot jump shots and hook shots at the beginning. But as Skip got better and the games grew closer, Howard would outmuscle his precocious apprentice, backing him down into the post for easy baskets.

In three cutthroat games Wise played against his mentor when no one else was in the gym, the main rule, above all others—a rule that Howard would employ years later when he put the same time and energy into teaching Muggsy Bogues and Reggie Williams how to play—was that Skip was never allowed to call a foul.

"He used to beat me to death," said Wise. "I started getting smarter and wouldn't drive to the basket as much so he didn't have as many chances to foul me. So I started developing a serious outside shot. Then, he'd respond by hitting my arms when I'd take those long jumpers, but I wasn't allowed to call a foul. I used to moan and complain and sometimes, to be honest, I'd be in tears. Mr. Howard didn't care. He'd actually be more physical with me if I started crying. But when I got to high school, I realized the purpose in all of that."

All of those brutal and physically intimidating games of one-on-one allowed Skip to develop the ability to absorb contact and still be able to concentrate on making his shots. And by being forced to operate far away from the basket on the perimeter, Wise developed a better shooting range than most players.

When he graduated from middle school, Skip Wise was 5 foot 11. By the beginning of his first basketball season at Dunbar High in 1972, he'd sprouted to 6 foot 3.

By the start of his junior year, Skip stood 6 foot 5 with a style modeled on his idol, Earl Monroe. His smooth showmanship and flair conspired with his unbelievably advanced skills to hypnotize crowds. An offensive wunderkind, he was notorious for his chest-high dribble, where the ball resembled a yo-yo at the end of an invisible string. His exceptional quickness, and his uncannily accurate jump shot, with range that extended far from the basket, made him virtually unstoppable. At Dunbar home games, the overflowing crowd routinely chanted "Layup!" whenever he pulled up for his jump shot. Deafening roars of "Honey Dip! Honey Dip! Honey Dip!" accompanied him wherever he played.

In 1973 and 1974, Wise led the Dunbar Poets to forty-seven consecutive victories, none more memorable than the highly anticipated matchup with Washington, DC's DeMatha Catholic High School during his junior season.

DeMatha, coached by the legendary Morgan Wootten, brought a powerful team in the midst of its own forty-three-game winning streak, headlined by Adrian Dantley, a 6-foot-5, 228-pound man-child considered the best prep player in the country. But Wise lit up Dantley and his heralded team for 39 points, with a fourth-quarter shooting display that today would headline an ESPN highlight reel. The crowd, 8,500 strong, was whipped into a state of delirium, chanting "Honey Dip! Honey Dip!" as Wise made one improbable shot after another. Had the 3-point line been in existence, Wise's total would have approached 50. Dunbar's 85–71 victory sent shock waves through the basketball establishment, and Wise's performance that day has become a tale passed down from generation to generation.

"Baltimore always had some very good talent, but people didn't know that," said Wise. "They thought Philly, DC, and New York was where all the talent was. When we spanked DeMatha, that's when Baltimore and Dunbar High School jumped into the national realm of things. And that team was mostly comprised of kids who had no interest in basketball until they met Mr. Howard at the rec center. The city started getting a lot more publicity, all the big-time college coaches started showing up, and I just happened to be fortunate enough to have a part in that."

After his sparkling performance against DeMatha, Skip's celebrity was no longer confined to the Lafayette Projects and East Baltimore. Mayor William Donald Schaeffer's face lit up when Skip walked into city hall with his teammates to celebrate their undefeated seasons. City councilmen elbowed one another for their own opportunities to have their pictures taken with him. And there were others who wanted a piece of Skip, guys who now began taking him shopping for fancy clothes, shoes, and jewelry, who began introducing him to stunningly curvaceous women while also sliding hundred-dollar bills in his pocket. These guys were businessmen who understood economic potential and how an investment could possibly pay dividends down the road. They also happened to be the powerful drug lords who controlled the city's heroin trade.

"When Skip was at Dunbar, I was back in Baltimore, coaching the varsity basketball team at Edmondson High School, where I also coached varsity baseball and was an assistant with the varsity football team," said Wade. "I was amazed at Skip's talent. He was such a tremendous player and you could see such a bright future for him. But the street agents got to him, and you could see him becoming more and more flamboyant, not just the way he played but with the clothes he wore and the way that he carried himself."

Like many plugged into the East Side grapevine, Wade heard that Wise was being seen around town hanging out in various nightclubs with major drug lords like "Little Melvin" Williams, who would go on to star many years later in the acclaimed HBO series *The Wire* as a concerned church deacon, and Marty Gross. He noticed the fancy jewelry and expensive coats, shoes, and outfits that Skip was stepping out in.

"I was concerned for Skip because not only did I hear the chatter about the money he was getting, who he was hanging around with, and all the dirty recruiting where some colleges were offering all types of illegal inducements, but I also knew about the character of the guys he was hanging out with and what they were doing. You always wanted to see kids be able to succeed, especially Skip because his talent was so immense and his future was so bright. He had the potential to be an outstanding pro if he kept his nose clean and did the right things. And I wanted to reach out to him; I thought maybe I'd be able to help him. Because you could see that he was heading down the wrong path."

Skip invigorated a moribund Clemson University basketball program that returned to the national rankings immediately upon his arrival in 1975. He became the first freshman ever in the ACC to be named a First Team All-Conference performer. After his outstanding freshman season at Clemson, in which he scorched the likes of celebrated guards John Lucas at the University of Maryland and Phil Ford at the University of North Carolina, Honey Dip signed a contract with the Baltimore Claws of the upstart American Basketball Association. But Wise, as many people would later learn when his Clemson coach Tates Locke published a tell-all book, *Caught in the Net*, had been compromised and commoditized from the moment he signed with Clemson. To make matters worse, Wise had already developed a drug habit while still in his teens.

When the Claws folded before finishing the preseason, the promise of Wise's six-figure contract evaporated. He auditioned for the Golden State Warriors and San Antonio Spurs, but his heroin addiction derailed his professional prospects. Terry Pluto, in his book about the American Basketball Association, *Loose Balls*, tells how a Golden State Warriors coach found Wise shivering on the locker room floor during tryouts, going through heroin withdrawal. Skip returned to East Baltimore's playgrounds, playing in pickup games shortly before vanishing into his addiction. Instead of his name appearing in newspaper headlines because of his basketball exploits, he began popping up on the police blotter and court dockets with regularity.

"I got down on my hands and knees and begged Skip to stay in school," his former coach at Dunbar, Sugar Cain, told the *Baltimore Sun* in 1977. "I told him he was making the biggest mistake of his life. I didn't think he was ready for the pros. You want to sit down and cry, it makes you so sad."

Wise spent the prime years of his athletic life tearing up prison basketball tournaments, watching longingly from jailhouse recreation rooms as NBA telecasts reintroduced him to players he had dominated during his one college season. He had once been a source of pride at the Lafayette Rec Center, where Leon Howard would tell the younger promising players, including preteens like Tyrone Bogues and Reggie Williams, that if they wanted to be great, if they were willing to work hard in school and in basketball practice, they, too, could have the same bright future as Skip once had.

—

Even at a young age, Muggsy Bogues was known for his shiny bald head, vivacious smile, and laughter. Among his earliest group of friends, which included his future Dunbar teammates Reggie Williams, Darryl Wood, and Jerry White, he was considered the leader.

"I might have been the smallest kid around, but I was always in charge," said Bogues. "We rode our bikes all over the city. We had those old roller skates that you attached to your sneakers and sometimes we'd skate all day, grabbing car bumpers and hitching rides. I was fearless, always leading some activity, getting things moving. I was always the point guard."

As a kid, Bogues took his basketball with him everywhere. He slept with it, dribbled it up and down steps, and made obstacle courses of cardboard boxes, dribbling through them as fast as he could. In the heavy snow of winter, he, Williams, Wood, White, and their other friends would clear spots on the asphalt big enough for them to dribble and shoot.

"We'd play in the pouring rain and in the heat of summer, all day, every day," said Bogues. "If the rec center was open, we played there, and if it wasn't, we played in the streets. I'd follow my brothers or sister to their pickup games and watch. They never picked me because I was so small and that made me furious. So me, Reg, OJ, Jerry White, and our other friends would get some empty milk crates and tie them to a chain-link fence. We'd have our own games."

He and his friends spent the majority of their time in the recreation center. After school, they'd walk home, toss their books aside, and sprint over to the Lafayette Rec. Oftentimes, they'd arrive before it opened and wait until Mr. Howard came to unlock the doors. The boys quickly proved that they were good enough to play on the team that would compete against the city's other neighborhood centers.

"Mr. Howard took an interest in us and invested so much of his time," said Reggie Williams. "He'd have me and Muggsy, and a couple of other kids who he thought had some potential, in the gym with him, putting us through all types of drills and training sessions. He'd tell us to get there early, before he opened the center, or he'd keep us late, after he had closed up and sent everybody else home. We'd be dribbling around chairs and practicing all the time."

Because Bogues was so short, Howard would stand in front of him with a broomstick that he held high in the air, instructing him to shoot over the top of it. Howard taught his boys the value of rebounding and passing, how to run an effective offensive attack, and numerous defensive strategies. He taught them the inherent advantage of shooting the ball off the backboard, along with an array of other subtle pointers that would expand their own individual skill sets, depending on their strengths and weaknesses.

"We ate that stuff up," said Williams. "And he would play us one-on-one. That was always the highlight. And the thing was, nobody could beat him! He was this short, stubby guy, but his jump shot never missed. He had all these head fakes and pump fakes, and he'd use his shoulders and forearms to push off and create just enough space to get his shot off. The biggest thing that we all talked about and looked forward to was being able to beat Mr. Howard one day."

Muggsy Bogues paid Coach Howard the highest compliment. "He had me dribbling with just my fingertips, working on crossovers and pivots and spin moves, while mastering the ability to change directions at top speeds. He taught me so much."

When Bogues stopped in to see Howard after his first few games as Dunbar's starting point guard, they talked about those earlier years and the fun times they had spent in the oasis of the recreation center.

They were both pleased that things were going so well for the Dunbar Poets.

CHAPTER SIX

"Games Were Like a Vacation"

EARLY DURING THE '81–'82 season, Bob Wade needed to deal with a problem concerning David Wingate right after the team's opening games. The senior, Coach Wade had learned, had been coming to school consistently late, and his first-period English teacher, Mrs. McMillan, had complained about it to Mrs. Woodland, the principal.

But there was an explanation for his lateness: "I never talked to my teachers in school about what was going on with me at home," said Wingate. "I felt comfortable talking with Coach Wade, and he knew what was going on. Mrs. McMillan thought I was trying to be slick, but she didn't know that my mom was paralyzed and that, a lot of times, in the morning, I had to get her situated before going to school."

A few years prior, when Wingate was fifteen and beginning his first year of high school, his mother had been a cafeteria worker in the Baltimore City Public Schools system. She walked into the hospital one day because of severe stomach pains, and during what was supposed to be a routine surgical procedure, a nerve was accidentally severed, causing her to become permanently paralyzed from the waist down. David Wingate Sr., David's father, had to work varying shifts as a foreman at the Harbison-Walker brick factory, so David and his sister, Shirley, were suddenly thrust into the role of their mother's caretakers. Shirley worked as a nurse's assistant at Stella Maris, a local health-care provider. Once their mother became confined to a wheelchair, Shirley was forced to work long weekend shifts to care for her mother during the week. "Sometimes, when Shirley had to leave the house on some mornings," said Wingate, "I was responsible for cooking my mother breakfast, giving her insulin shots, and carrying her up and down the steps. That was my job. I had to make sure she was settled, had her medication, had something to eat, and then I would roll on out to school."

Wingate was hesitant to talk freely with others about his increased responsibilities, fearing that they might laugh at him. Every day, by dusk, his mother wanted to be upstairs in her room. And one of his jobs was to carry her up there. He'd be outside at the park playing ball, and even if he was right in the middle of a good game, he'd jump over the fence and sprint down the hill to get home before dark, while his friends would stand perplexed.

"I'd come tearing around that corner, and my mother would be right at the front door, looking for me," said Wingate. "I had more responsibility than the average teenager, and sometimes I felt like I was missing out on all the fun that the other kids were having."

While at Dunbar, during summer vacations, when his friends were hanging out late and going to parties, he was required to be home by 11:00 p.m. He'd get very angry, wondering why his friends could be having so much fun, while he felt like he was being punished.

"I was really mad and couldn't figure out the purpose in all of that," said Wingate. "But I recently went back to the old neighborhood. And all of those people that she was trying to keep me away from, people I wanted to be hanging out and going to meet girls with at the parties and stuff, all of them are either locked up, strung out on drugs, or dead now. At the time, I'd be asking myself, 'Why is my mom so strict? Why does she treat me like this?' But she knew what she was doing."

When Wade spoke with Mrs. McMillan and informed her of Wingate's circumstances, the teacher agreed not to penalize him for arriving late or even missing a class here and there. She also arranged for him to work privately with her to make sure he was up to speed on all missed work and assignments. But Wingate was not a selfless innocent, either. He had a mischievous side and skipped out of school to cut classes from time to time.

"Early in the season, we were in the locker room as Coach was handing out new pairs of sneakers from a shipment that he'd received from one of the sneaker companies," said Eric Green, the star quarterback and baseball player who was one of the Dunbar Poet role players. "And David came in with this goofy walk, smiling and joking. When he walked up to Coach Wade to get his sneakers, Wade looked up at him and took off his glasses. We all stepped back because when Coach took off his glasses, we knew what that meant. He jumped up, grabbed Gate by the collar, and lifted him clean off the ground. Gate started talking real fast, saying, 'What did I do? What did I do?' And Coach said, 'Dammit! You know what you did. You want to mess up your future and lose your scholarships? If you hook another class, I'm gonna kick your ass!' Today, people might not understand that type of discipline, but Coach wasn't being abusive or trying to intimidate us. He'd earned the respect to be able to do that because we knew that he really cared about us and didn't want us to mess up later in life."

College recruiters were paying attention to Wingate. North Carolina State, Georgia, Georgetown, Maryland, and Providence were among the many schools offering him a scholarship.

"During my senior year, I really wanted to play at either Georgia or Maryland," said Wingate. "Dominique Wilkins hosted me on my visit to the University of Georgia, and we had a ball. Georgetown and Providence were pushing hard, though. I'd never heard of Georgetown before until Patrick Ewing got there. He was a college freshman during my final season at Dunbar, and they really started making some major noise. And when Big John Thompson, the head coach at Georgetown, comes walking into your house for a recruiting visit, he makes a very extraordinary impression."

"My mother didn't know anything about basketball," Wingate continued. "As a matter of fact, she hadn't ever seen me play. With her being in a wheelchair and in her physical condition, it was difficult for her to get to a game. And one northeastern college wanted me and Gary Graham to come there together as a package deal. But on our recruiting visit there, we went out to dinner with all of these businessmen who were boosters for the school's basketball team. And those guys were scary. They were talking in hand signals, whispering into each other's ears and stuff, wearing diamond pinky rings, pulling us aside and asking us what it was going to take for us to go there. Maybe I watched *The Godfather* too much, but I was afraid of those guys. I told Gary, 'Man, let's get outta here. I ain't gonna be playing no ball for the Mafia.' We bailed out on that recruiting visit a day early."

Wingate's mother, despite knowing nothing about basketball and having never seen her son play in high school, wouldn't talk to him about any school other than Georgetown. Her face would light up when she mentioned John Thompson, who she felt was the exact type of role model, similar to Coach Wade at Dunbar, that David needed.

Gary Graham, the team's other senior star, was also being deluged with recruiting mail.

"We all thought about going to Maryland, especially with my older brother Ernie having played there," said Graham. "They had the highest visibility to us because that's who we saw on television and in the newspapers the most, being in Baltimore. Jim Valvano at North Carolina State was recruiting me really heavily, and I thought about them a lot, too, because one of my brothers had a good relationship with Valvano. Providence, Penn State, and UNLV were also in the mix. John Thompson, the coach at Georgetown, had been very close with my family since he tried to recruit my brother Ernie when he was in high school. He used to stop by my house and have dinner all the time, even after Ernie decided to go to Maryland. He had enough guards at Georgetown and he really wanted Gate. But John Thompson was trying to get me to go to Providence. I didn't realize it at the time, but he had gone to Providence. And Dave Gavitt, the commissioner of the Big East, had once coached there. The Big East was really starting to become a factor, so Coach Thompson, even though he wasn't recruiting me to go to Georgetown, was trying to make sure that Providence got some talented players and that the best players in the region stayed to play in the Big East."

Wade's involvement in Graham's recruiting process was minimal compared to how he watched over Wingate. Wade knew that with Graham's brothers having been through the process, his parents were sufficiently well versed to make a good decision. But Wade worried about Wingate. He felt that David's recruitment required his attention because the family could easily be misled by the false promises that many college coaches make.

Wade also provided job opportunities to some of his players to earn some money, employing them at Northwest Plaza Liquors, the store (in Baltimore parlance the "cut rate") of which he was a part-owner.

Wade would pick up some of his players and drive them to the job on weekends, where they'd work the cash register, sell lottery tickets, fill the refrigerators, sweep the floors, and stock the shelves. The players appreciated the opportunity to earn some money, but they also looked forward to spending time with their coach outside of school and basketball practice, where he was more like an actual dad and a friend.

"We listened to all of that because he didn't just talk the talk, he walked the walk," said Graham. "When some people said things, you didn't always trust and believe them, but when Coach Wade said something, you believed every word because you knew that he had lived it."

Reggie Williams would even sleep at Wade's home on some weekends.

"I'd sleep on the bottom of the bunk bed while his son Darryl slept on the top," said Williams. "On Monday mornings, we'd drop Darryl and his youngest son Darion off at their school and then we'd ride to Dunbar together. His interest in me, and all of his players, went beyond basketball. He was teaching us how to be a husband, a leader, a father, and how to work hard in order to succeed in life."

He might have been a friend or a dad off the court, but in the gym, especially after the Poet-Laker Invitational, Wade increased the pressure in practice. Five days after beating Lake Clifton, the Poets took a trip down the Baltimore–Washington Parkway to play McKinley Tech, one of the strongest public school teams in the District of Columbia.

During the first half of the game against McKinley Tech, Reggie Williams ran into foul trouble, forcing Wade to send Reggie Lewis into the game earlier than normal. At halftime, with the score tied at 22, Wade exploded in the locker room.

"You knew he was really mad when he'd yell at me and the assistant coach Lynn Badham, telling us to get the hell out of the locker room," said Marshall Goodwin, Wade's good friend who worked with the sherriff's department and served as the team's unofficial security guard.

"We jumped out on McKinley in the first quarter, but in the second quarter, we just couldn't hit any shots," said Bogues. "Coach was so angry because he knew that we were much better than we were playing. And he made that very clear, in his own unique way. We knew that when he threw his towel and stomped out of the locker room, just leaving us sitting there looking at ourselves, that it was time to go to work."

Reggie Williams, who'd only scored 5 points in the opening half, took it upon himself to lift his squad out of its lethargy. Behind Williams's 16-point second-half scoring binge, the Poets outscored McKinley 31–14 over the final two quarters and coasted to a 53–36 victory. In the fourth quarter, Dunbar held McKinley to 4 points. David Wingate was the team's second leading scorer with 14 points, while Reggie Lewis played admirably in his first extended action of the season, scoring 8. Wade's halftime explosion had produced the desired effect. The team had responded.

But with more than a full week before their next game, the team could not sense any of their coach's pleasure with how they responded in the second half against McKinley. Wade knew that with only two games left before they departed for a tournament in New York, he wanted to ramp up the pressure in practice. And that meant pestering his players even more than he normally would.

"We worked our tails off in practice because we never wanted to disappoint Coach Wade," said Eric Green. "We were all afraid of him coming down on us, and that motivated us to play harder than we ever knew that we could play. Those drills where we took charges were vicious. Everybody left practices with bloody knees and elbows. And if there was a loose ball, we all tried to jump on that thing like it was a goal-line fumble in a football game. Games to us were like a vacation because our practices were so unbelievably hard."

Reggie Williams said that he and his Lafayette Rec buddies weren't bothered by Wade yelling at them. "Nobody yelling and screaming and cursing at us was going to frighten us. Shoot, on the street, we cursed more than he did."

As Muggsy Bogues observed, he and his friends had bigger problems than being yelled at in basketball practice. "We'd be walking home from school and have to dive under cars or hop over fences when we heard gunshots and saw people shooting at one another. We saw some terrifying stuff, so Coach Wade yelling and hollering, that wasn't a big deal to us."

Wade tried to find the right way to motivate Reggie Lewis, who he knew had innate talent.

"You don't have a jump shot," Wade would tell Lewis. "And you can't dribble."

But the coach would smile when, after practice, Lewis would

stay late, setting up cones and chairs, devising his own obstacle courses to dribble through as he worked on his ball handling and jump shot. When he made a jump shot during a game, the quiet newcomer and sixth man would run past the bench, look at his coach, and say, "I have a jumper!"

"Truck was very driven to prove to me that he had that shot, that he could dribble and score if we needed him to," said Wade. "He might have been extremely quiet and hard to read, but he was so determined."

But after one exhausting practice, Lewis had had enough. While his teammates joked around in the locker room as they dressed to go home, he hastily put on his clothes and hurried out into the brisk winter evening. Instead of taking the bus or catching a ride home with Tim Dawson's dad or Sheriff Marshall Goodwin, he walked, emotions bubbling inside of him. When he arrived at home, his mother could see that her son was upset. Reggie told her that he was going to quit the basketball team. Before heading out to her second job working at a local bar, after a full day spent doing manual labor at a paper cup factory, she urged her son to be patient and not give up.

"Truck was not the only guy who thought about quitting the team, I can attest to that," said Keith Wallace. "I remember during one of those first practices I threw a sweet behind-the-back pass that resulted in a layup. I did get a little fancy with it and could probably have made a simpler pass. But Coach yanked me to the sidelines and said, 'We don't showboat here.' There were a number of instances where I thought about going someplace else. And I'm sure that all of the other guys, at one point or another, after having been screamed at by Coach, thought the same thing."

On Saturday, December 19, the Poets took out their frustrations on Baltimore Polytechnic Institute, one of the city's elite academic public schools, thrashing them, 77–47. Reggie Williams scored 28 points and pulled down 10 rebounds while Wingate chipped in with 20 points. That next Tuesday, they destroyed Mergenthaler Vocational Tech, known around the city as Mervo, 93–50. Williams again paced the Poets with 33 points and 12 rebounds while Wingate added 26 points. The vaunted forward tandem, along with Gary Graham, combined for 71 points over the first three quarters before Wade sent in his substitutes.

The Poets were ready for New York.

Dunbar High School.

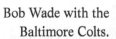

Bob Wade with the
Baltimore Colts.

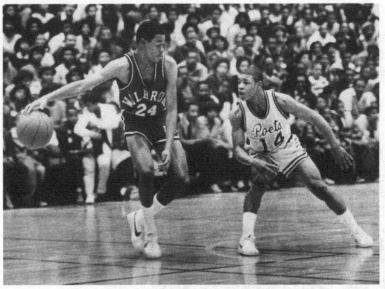

Muggsy Bogues playing defense.

David Wingate goes up for a
running one-hander.

Reggie Lewis shooting over a Lake Clifton defender.

Reggie Williams
pump fakes before
taking his shot.

Bob Wade on the bench
in his typical fiery mode
during the Capital Classic.

Keith James driving the ball on a fast break.

Tim Dawson (41) goes up for a rebound.

Muggsy Bogues and Gary Graham, Dunbar's dynamic backcourt.

David Wingate soars
for a dunk.

Reggie Lewis (31),
shooting over a defender
in the paint.

Reggie Williams fakes
two Walbrook defenders
before shooting.

Leon Howard, longtime
head of the Lafayette
Recreational Center.

Muggsy Bogues, Darryl Wood, and Reggie Lewis *(left to right)* with Coach Wade (behind Wood) at the scorer's table, waiting to enter a game. Assistant Coach Lynn Badham sits next to Coach Wade.

The Dunbar Poets with their city championship trophies for the 1981–82 season at Morgan State University.

CHAPTER SEVEN

"I'm Gonna Shoot Yo' Ass!"

AS THE HOLIDAY SEASON arrived and the public schools went on winter break, the Dunbar Poets were preparing for a trip to New York to play in the Harlem Holiday Classic. But much of Baltimore had little to celebrate that Christmas.

Thousands of employees were being laid off and furloughed at the city's Bethlehem Steel plants and finishing mills. The behemoth Beth Steel industrial complex at Sparrows Point stretched for four miles from end to end. At one point, it symbolized America's manufacturing might. The city's unemployment rate at the close of 1981 was slightly above 11 percent and steadily rising. The A&P supermarkets were scheduled to close all of their city stores by early January. Baltimore's aging General Motors assembly plant on Broening Highway, which produced midsized, rear-wheel drive Monte Carlo and Malibu models, was also being hit with heavy layoffs.

Police and crime statistics showed that assaults, robberies, murders, and other violent crimes had increased substantially since the year prior.

"That was a difficult time for a lot of blue-collar workers and their families in Baltimore," said Wade. "People who once had steady, dependable work in the plants, factories, and mills were losing their jobs and a way of life they'd known for close to two generations. At one time, you could make a good, respectable living without needing to have a high school or college education if you were lucky enough to have a union job. It was hard work, but people took pride in that work ethic, bought homes, raised families, tried to send their kids off to college. But those days were quickly coming to an end. You could see that the community, which was once so vibrant, was now suffering."

But in the midst of East Baltimore's growing struggles, the community rallied around the Poets with more fervor than ever. People tussling with financial hardships, unemployment, a widening recession, and frightening crime and homicide rates, left the gym after watching the Poets feeling better about their own lives, encouraged by the team's originality, rare ingenuity, and burgeoning talent.

The Dunbar players may not have understood the ominous economic situation, but they had long been familiar with hard times. But knowing about hard times and being burdened by them were two distinct issues.

"Even though we grew up in a place that many people on the outside thought was a terrible environment, it was the greatest place in the world to us growing up," said Reggie Williams. "We were happy kids and teenagers. We weren't blind; we could see some really negative stuff going on around us, but we were almost shielded from that. I can look back now and see how my mom was struggling, but we never felt like things were bad. Muggs and I and the rest of the guys were happy-go-lucky kids, just playing ball and having fun. That was a great Christmas for us."

———

On December 25, 1981, all of the Poets had to cut short their normal Christmas celebration and report to the school at 7:30 a.m. At 8:00 a.m., their chartered bus pulled out of East Baltimore, heading toward I-95 for the four-hour ride up north.

"That was the first time going out of town for all of us, in terms of playing in a big tournament like that," said Reggie Williams. "We were excited to get up there and play our game. We felt like Baltimore was still looked down on, that people thought that DC, Philadelphia, and New York were where the best basketball players came from. We felt like we were the forgotten town. We had guys that we looked up to when we were growing up that played at Dunbar like Skip Wise, Larry Gibson, and Ernie Graham who did well on the big stage once they got to college. But we felt like Baltimore still wasn't given its proper respect. Going up to New York, we wanted to get our names out there. We wanted to go up there and dominate and let the whole country know that Baltimore took a backseat to no one when it came to basketball talent."

"We were more excited about going up to Harlem to play some really good teams than we were about Christmas," said David Wingate. "I had never been out of town before to play in a big high school tournament like that, and this was my first time going up to the big city. The energy on that bus ride was something else. We were laughing and joking around, but all of us were ready to get on that basketball court up in New York."

In the front of the bus, Bob Wade was also in a good mood.

He'd had a great Christmas Eve, though an abbreviated one, with his family. After the team had won its previous two games by a combined 73 points, he felt that his boys were ready to face the stiff competition they'd be matched up against in the Harlem Holiday Classic.

"I was still a little bit nervous about how we'd respond if we found ourselves in a tight game over the final few minutes. But I wasn't as concerned as I was when the season started, because Muggsy had already shown me that there wasn't a better ball handler and point guard in the country who could handle pressure. Mr. Badham and I talked a little strategy during the ride to New York, but for the most part, we were just as loose as the kids."

The promoter of the Harlem Holiday Classic had given Wade the address of where his team would be lodged and made it seem as if there were few better accommodations to be had in the city. But when Mr. Parran, the owner of the small company that handled all of Dunbar's out-of-town transportation needs, pulled his bus up in front of 180 West 135th Street, Wade thought they must have been lost.

"When we got to Harlem and Mr. Parran assured me that this was the address of where we were staying, I couldn't believe it," said Wade. "The promoter of the event lied to me and told me we'd be staying at a very nice hotel that was very close to the City College of New York, where the tournament was being held. He was right about being close to City College, but he wildly exaggerated the part about it being a very nice hotel."

The promoter had told Wade that the Poets and the other teams from out of town would be lodged in the historic Claude McKay Residence. Although it was designated a national historic landmark in 1976, the building where McKay, one of the luminaries of the Harlem Renaissance literary movement, had once resided in the 1940s was now the Harlem YMCA. And in the late winter of 1981, it had none of the charm it once possessed during the Harlem Renaissance.

"When we pulled up and stopped in front of the Harlem Y, I could almost see smoke coming out of Coach Wade's ears," said Badham. "We told the guys to stay on the bus, and the two of us went inside to check the place out. As soon as we walked in, Coach Wade became furious. If that promoter had been within arm's reach, right then and there, I'd hate to think what Bob might have done to him. He was beyond pissed."

Mr. Parran, who had been driving Wade and his Dunbar teams to their out-of-town trips for years, was like a member of the Dunbar family. He, Badham, and Wade, outside of earshot of the boys, debated about whether they should stay in New York to play in the tournament. Initially, Wade was adamant that they should not. He was ready to go home. Parran and Badham pointed out that the boys were well grounded; they followed the rules. Even though the accommodations were crappy and the distractions looked daunting, they were optimistic that the boys, under their supervision, could handle it. Wade calmed down slightly, but he remained livid. After some more discussion, he grudgingly decided that the team would stay and play in the tournament.

"Gentlemen, I need your attention," Wade announced at the front of the bus. "Our housing accommodations are not what were promised, and quite honestly, I'm very pissed off right now. I'm almost tempted to turn this bus around and go back home and say to hell with this tournament. But we're up here, and we'll make the best of it. Let's go in and get settled in our rooms. We'll meet right back downstairs in the lobby in fifteen minutes."

When the boys walked into the Y's vestibule and got a glance of the surroundings, the excitement and laughter from the bus ride was replaced with the questioning stares they shot at one another. "Man, we were looking at one another like, '*Where. The. Hell. Are. We!!!???*'" said Bogues. "That place was grimy, bizarre, and rowdy. And there were all of these homosexuals. I mean, a lot of them, hanging out in the lobby, and they looked comfortable, like they actually lived there. They were looking at us and smiling and waving. I mean, we were kids from the Baltimore projects and we weren't scared of nothing or anybody. But we'd never seen or been in any environment like this. It was crazy."

"That place was a hellhole," said Reggie Williams. "It was the worst place I'd ever been to. I felt like the homeless guys that were sleeping outside in the cardboard boxes had better accommodations. It was just awful. Coach Wade wasn't the only one who was pissed. We were like, 'Okay, ya'll are gonna put us up in this dump?' We felt disrespected and told one another that we were going to take it out on those New York teams that we'd be playing in the tournament."

After going to their rooms and dropping off their belongings, the team met in the lobby, where they were given the choice of hanging around the Y together or going down to Madison Square Garden to watch the New York Knicks play the New Jersey Nets in a Christmas Day matinee game.

The players who chose the game were treated to a thrilling back-and-forth contest, despite the fact that neither team was very good. The Nets, who'd only won ten of their first twenty-six games, defeated the Knicks 96–95, whose record was an equally dismal 12–27.

"I went to the Knicks game with Truck, Amos, Keith, and Karl Wallace and a few of the other guys," said Wingate. "I'd never been to an NBA game before. We jumped back on the bus and Mr. Parran drove us down to Madison Square Garden. The whole ride, I was looking out the window at the huge city with all of these buildings and people racing everywhere. I was amazed. Boy, we had a good time, watching the game and eating hot dogs and getting sodas. That was such a great experience, being up there together like that."

"The Nets had Buck Williams, Albert King, and Len Elmore, who had all gone to the University of Maryland," said Wingate. "They were recruiting me pretty heavily and, at the time, that's where I thought I wanted to play my college ball. And we were watching Michael Ray Richardson for the Knicks and giving one another high fives because he was amazing. I was sitting there thinking about playing college ball the next year, and that I'd be playing in places like Madison Square Garden. I was thinking that I might have a chance to be a pro one day if I worked hard and kept getting better. That was very exciting to me, to feel like I was getting very close to being able to play ball on the biggest stage."

After Wingate, Reggie Lewis, and the other guys returned from the Knicks game, they had another exciting experience, besides watching the Knicks' Sugar Ray Richardson, to share with their teammates.

"We were walking out of Madison Square Garden and this guy ran up to us and asked us if we would help him," said Keith Wallace. "We were all wearing our Dunbar jackets and I don't know why he thought we'd help him, but he said some guys were getting ready to fight him and he needed our help. We just all stood there looking at him, when a bunch of guys ran up on him and started whooping his behind. We all just started running toward the bus and as we kept looking back at the guy, those other guys looked like they were tearing the fur off him. It was crazy! We laughed about that the whole bus ride back to the Y."

The rest of the players chose to explore the neighborhood in search of something good to eat. They walked down to 125th Street, hit up some of the local food spots, and, with some of the pocket change they'd brought along with them, did some shopping while soaking up the local flavor.

Early that evening, the boys decided to go out and explore another part of the city together. But Reggie Williams decided that he wanted to take a shower first. The boys and coaches were all situated in six separate rooms spread throughout the sixth floor. After walking to the bathroom in his towel, Reggie Williams came sprinting back into the room he shared with Muggsy and OJ.

"Reggie ran back to our room, and, man, he was talking so fast, it was hard to understand him at first," said Bogues. "Reg hardly ever talked sometimes, so he had our undivided attention because he looked upset. He said there weren't any individual showers, just one big community shower in the bathroom. He was angry and said that as soon as he started washing himself up, some gay guys came into the bathroom and were trying to talk to him while he was naked in the shower. He said, 'M-m-m-man, they-they-they was in there l-l-l-lookin' at my stuff!' He was struggling to get his words out. We started laughing, and Reg didn't think that was funny at all."

Muggsy and Reggie went around to everyone else's rooms to let them know what was going on. All of the players made a pact that if one person in the room had to go to the bathroom, everybody in the room would go together. They were still joking around about the situation, but the giggling subsided after they walked into the bathroom together a little bit later, where they found notes written on the mirrors in lipstick, telling them that some of the residents thought they were cute and instructing them to go to certain rooms if they wanted to have some fun.

"After that, nobody was going off on their own to walk around, or do anything in the building by themselves," said Bogues.

Ever the leader, it was Muggsy who came up with the boys' plan for the evening.

"Somebody told us that we should go out at night and check out this place called 'The Deuce,'" said Bogues. "So at around seven o'clock, we all hopped into three separate cabs and went down to 42nd Street and Times Square. Now that place was *really* crazy."

Today, the area around 42nd Street and Times Square is vibrant and a more family- and tourist-friendly destination with thriving retail stores and movie theaters. But back in the early 1980s, it was a blighted, hostile landscape, a stretch of urban decay and vice proliferated with rat-infested XXX theaters, peep shows, and sex and pornography stores, among other dubious businesses. The area was the domain of pimps, prostitutes, drug addicts, and any number of thugs and hustlers working street angles.

"We walked around down there for a few hours and had a ball," said Bogues. "We weren't bad kids and didn't get into any trouble, but that whole scene was hilarious to us. You could tell it was kind of dangerous and shady, but there were about thirteen of us strolling around out there together. We were pretty deep and felt like if something jumped off, we'd be able to handle ourselves."

One player who decided to take a momentary walk on the wild side was David Wingate.

"We walked by one of the peep shows and the bouncer was like, 'Hey, for five dollars, ya'll can come on in and check out the best girls in the city,'" said Wingate. "Me and Eric Green paid five dollars and went on in. And as soon as we walked in the door, we didn't see much, because they kicked us out and told us that we were too young. They said if we really wanted to get in, we'd have to kick in another five dollars. We told them to give us our money back, but they wouldn't. They just laughed and said they'd give us an I.O.U. Man, the guys who stayed outside and didn't get hustled out of their five dollars clowned and joked on us about that all night long."

The boys were back in their rooms that evening in time for curfew, talking basketball, excited to get the tournament started that next day.

"Late that night, right before Mr. Badham and I were about to go to bed," said Coach Wade, "we looked out of our window where we could see into a courtyard. We could see Gary Graham standing by his open window, directly across from us, looking around from left to right. We said, 'What is he doing?' and as we got up to look closer, he was peeing out the window. We went over to his room, and he apologized and said, 'Mr. Wade, my roommates are in bed and I wasn't going into that bathroom by myself. I'm sorry, but I had to go bad!' We laughed about that until we fell asleep."

The next afternoon, on Saturday, December 26, the Poets took the quick bus ride from the Harlem Y over to the campus of the City College of New York on 138th Street and Convent Avenue. The Nat Holman Gymnasium was bubbling with animated fans who packed the stands. The team arrived a few hours before their scheduled game against Harlem's Rice High School, hoping to scout some of the teams that they might play in the coming days. As soon as they sat down in a vacant section high up in the bleachers, Wade was irate once again as he smelled marijuana smoke all around them. He stood up and said he was taking everyone home.

"We just said, 'Hey, Coach, we're here now, it don't make any sense to go home, so let's just get it going and do what we came here to do: win this thing and bring that championship trophy back to Baltimore,'" said Reggie Williams.

As the Poets took the court to warm up, they were booed mercilessly by the hometown crowd cheering for Rice. When the fans saw Muggsy announced during the starting lineups, snickers and laughter came raining down from the stands.

"When they got to giggling at Muggsy, I said to myself, 'Oh shit, they have no idea that the more they giggle, the more that Rice team was going to get its ass torn up,'" said Reggie Williams. "I looked at him, and you could see the focus and determination on his face. I told him, 'You know what you gotta do, Little Fella.' And he looked at me and said, 'They in trouble, Big Fella.'"

"I was used to that reception whenever I played in a place where people hadn't seen me before," said Bogues. "They would just laugh at me and think that, because of my height, they were going to have an easy game. Well, after that first quarter, nobody was laughing at me anymore."

After opening up a 24–12 lead, Dunbar was never threatened. The backcourt of Bogues and Graham both scored 12 points while also getting 5 steals apiece. Muggsy also dished out a plethora of dazzling assists that drew gasps from the crowd as Tim Dawson, David Wingate, and Reggie Williams dunked all over the hapless Rice defenders. Williams was a force of nature with his 25 points and 13 rebounds, and David Wingate chipped in with 10 points as the Poets cruised to a 77–51 victory.

"New York is known for its point guard play, and they got treated to a special show by Muggsy," said Wade. "They'd never seen a player of his stature dominate a game like that. When he was sitting on the bench in the fourth quarter while our second and third teams played, people in the crowd were screaming for us to put him back in. He opened a lot of eyes during that game."

The next evening, in the tournament semifinal game, the Poets ran their record to 8–0 after beating New Jersey's East Orange High School 66–55. Reggie Williams scored 12 of his team's first 13 points en route to a dominating performance, exploding for 31 points and 10 rebounds in only three quarters. He was forced to sit out most of the fourth quarter with foul trouble, but Reggie Lewis picked up the slack in his absence during the final period, scoring 8 points.

"Whenever I got substituted out or got into foul trouble, you could almost sense the other team getting excited, getting their hopes up," said Williams. "But when Truck came in the game, they realized that they had to deal with another Reggie, and he had some serious game as well. Teams and opposing fans would be shocked at our depth. We firmly believed that our second group of five was better than many good teams' starting five. We seriously felt like after us and Calvert Hall, the third best team in Baltimore was on our bench. That's how good our substitutes were and the type of chemistry we had. People might have gotten initially excited when me or Muggsy or Wingate had to go to the bench, but our subs were going to give out the same type of ass whooping that we gave out. When they realized that, they were shocked with the weapons we had on the bench."

The suffocating Dunbar defense was spearheaded by Muggsy's seven steals and Wingate's six blocked shots. Williams also asserted himself defensively during the decisive second quarter, blocking three straight shots as the Poets went into halftime with a 28–19 lead. Wingate added 10 points while Bogues chipped in with 9, along with another phenomenal passing exhibition.

In the championship game, the Poets would be matched up against the crowd favorite, Brooklyn's Alexander Hamilton High School, the Harlem Holiday Classic's defending champion.

"They had this guy named Sky Irvin, some little guy that could jump real high whom everybody was talking about," said Williams. "That's all we heard about while we were up there, Sky Irvin, and how we were going to have to deal with him when we played Alexander Hamilton. That got us excited. We were like, 'Okay, if he's the real deal, then bring him on!'"

But the Poets found that they also had to contend with some questionable officiating.

"It was evident early on during that championship game that Russ and Muggsy had targets on their backs," said Wade. "Not only was that crowd against us, it felt like the refs were as well. They were making phantom calls that were absolutely ridiculous."

Both Williams and Bogues were forced to sit out much of the second half with foul trouble. But the depth of the Dunbar bench was something that Alexander Hamilton, and the refs, could not account for.

"I couldn't believe the fouls they were calling on me and Russ," said Bogues. "That was tough, having to be on the bench for such a long period of time. But OJ came in and played great in the backcourt with Gary Graham, who was fantastic. Truck and Keith James came in off the bench and were super as well. We were up by ten points at the end of the third quarter, and our defense was great. They only scored four points in the third quarter, but we just couldn't shake them and pull away."

Gary Graham scored 17 points, grabbed 10 rebounds, and dished out 7 assists while Wingate added 14 points and 12 rebounds. Reggie Williams, who'd scored 56 points in the tournament's first two games, had only 6 by the time Wade substituted him back in, saddled with 4 fouls, with less than four minutes remaining in the game. But when Alexander Hamilton cut the Poets' lead to 3 points with fifty-nine seconds left, it was Williams who calmly knocked down 4 free throws in the bonus situation to seal the victory.

Williams's game-clinching free throws, impressive as they were, followed a couple of free throws that were even more dramatic. David Wingate was in the midst of a late-game hot streak, hitting one difficult long-range jumper after another. When he was fouled on one shot with less than two minutes left on the clock, Wade called time-out. As Wingate was walking toward the bench, a spectator started yelling at him.

"This guy had been yelling at me all game," said Wingate. "He was a young guy, maybe in his early twenties. We were used to hostile crowds, so I didn't pay him much mind. But as I was walking to the bench, he called out to me. I'd normally ignore that type of stuff, but for some reason, I looked at him. He opened up his trench coat and showed me a gun that he had in his waistband. He said, 'Motherfucker, if you hit those free throws, I'm gonna shoot yo' ass!'"

As Wade was going over his late-game strategy, he noticed that Wingate was antsy and distracted.

"I looked at him and he looked scared," said Wade. "I'd never seen David look scared on the basketball court. I asked him what was wrong, and he pointed to the guy, who was sitting under the basket that we were shooting at, and told me what he said to him. I looked him square in the eyes and said, 'David, if you miss those free throws, I am going to shoot you. Who are you more afraid of, him or me? Don't worry about him. We'll take care of him. Just knock down your shots.'"

"I was sitting behind the bench with the group of Poet Followers that traveled to every Dunbar game," said Baltimore sheriff Marshall Goodwin, the team's volunteer security guard. "They chartered their own transportation and made it up to Harlem for that championship game. Coach Wade told me what happened, and I grabbed up about ten of the men from the Poet Followers who came up from Baltimore. I gave them the scoop, and we walked over to the basket that David was about to shoot at."

The Poet Followers stood on the baseline with their backs to the court, folded their arms, and stared at the guy in the trench coat.

"I walked up to the dude and whispered in his ear, 'Motherfucker, we ain't lettin' nobody do a damn thing to one of our kids,'" said Goodwin. "I told him, 'Whatever you got, bring it, 'cause we don't play that shit in Baltimore. And I guarantee, you are not prepared for what we will unleash on you if you start some shit up in here. So sit the fuck down and act like you have some sense.' He sat down, I stood right next to him, and the Poet Followers didn't see any of the rest of the game. They just stared at the dude. He didn't say shit for the rest of the game. There was no way we were going to let anybody mess with our kids. That dude picked the wrong people to mess with that day."

Reggie Williams finished with 10 points and 11 rebounds in Dunbar's 62–56 victory. Bogues scored 10 points, snatched 6 steals, and dished out 7 assists despite playing less than half of the game, and was named the tournament's Most Valuable Player.

"I remember after that championship game, some grown, and I mean some very, very sexy women mobbed us as we were celebrating," said Eric Green. "I didn't even play, and they were coming up to me like I just scored thirty points, telling me they wanted to come back to our hotel with us. We were like, 'Man! We need to come to New York more often!'"

"That was Muggsy's coming-out party up in New York," said Wade. "People outside of Baltimore hadn't seen him yet. Those New York people were shocked and amazed at how dominant

Muggs was. He electrified that crowd. They wanted their team to win, but those folks appreciated some great basketball, and they knew a terrific point guard when they saw one. When we were getting our trophies and they named him the MVP, those people gave him a standing ovation."

"Go to the locker room and change your clothes," Wade told his team after the trophy presentation. "Don't even take a shower. Just get dressed and get your asses on the bus so we can get the hell out of here."

"We were so hyped on that bus ride back to Baltimore," said Bogues. "It was about eleven o'clock at night when we pulled out of Manhattan and hit the turnpike. We were singing, dancing, laughing, cracking jokes, doing our cheers, just celebrating and having a great time. We had so much fun. And the bond we formed up there, it was hard to describe. We became even closer after that."

The celebration went on for about an hour. After the guys settled down, as Mr. Parran drove his bus through New Jersey, into Delaware, and on through Maryland, the only sounds to be heard were loud snores.

CHAPTER EIGHT

"Coach Wade Was Relentless"

THE TEAM HAD A day of rest on Tuesday, December 29, but they were right back in the gym on Wednesday.

"All of the team's practices were tough, but when the guys were on winter vacation and didn't have to worry about classes and homework, Coach's practices could really be vicious," said Goodwin. "Over the holidays, he got those guys in the gym early and drilled them mercilessly."

They practiced every day except Sunday before returning to their normal routine when school resumed on Monday, January 4. That winter was quickly proving to be one of the century's worst, with major snowstorms crippling the city on what seemed a weekly basis. But even Mother Nature could not alter the team's preparation.

"There was one day where the snow was literally knee high, and Coach Wade actually arranged for us to be picked up from our homes by the city dump trucks that were out there plowing the streets, so they could bring us to practice," said Tim Dawson. "Not only did that show how connected he was, to be able to arrange for something like that, it also showed that he was on a mission."

"I called up my friend Ray Short, who was the head of the Poets Followers group that supported us and traveled to every one of our away games," said Wade. "He was the director of the grounds shop for the Baltimore City Public Schools. I asked him if he could help me get some of the kids to practice during a blizzard. He said not to worry about it, that he would take care of it. I gave him the addresses of most of the kids, and when I got to the gym, everybody was there and we practiced."

"Coach was not going to let a blizzard stop us from practicing," said Reggie Williams. "I figured that I wouldn't be able to make it to practice, but Coach Wade sent somebody over to pick me up in this big Baltimore City pickup truck. I was like, 'Wow! The whole city is shut down and we're still having practice. This guy is something else.'"

With their rivals at Calvert Hall, the private school team that had outlasted them in the final game the year prior, also being undefeated, and having beaten some strong teams in Las Vegas during the Nike Holiday Classic, Baltimore City laid claim to having two of the top five high school basketball programs in the country. According to *Street & Smith's* magazine, Calvert Hall was ranked number one, followed by Camden High School in New Jersey at number two. The Dunbar Poets were climbing in the national rankings.

Bob Wade was eager to play Calvert Hall and avenge last year's loss, but they were not on the Poets' schedule for the '81–'82 season. He made sure that the Poets stayed focused on the task at hand. "We had three big games coming up against teams that were very good: Walbrook, Carver, and Lake Clifton. So I felt like my job was to make sure that they stayed motivated and hungry."

And yet, despite his best efforts, the Poets looked anything but hungry at the start of their first game back after the break on Saturday, January 9. Trailing Walbrook High School 15–13 after the first quarter, the boys were out of sync offensively. Shots that they would usually hit were off the mark, passes were dropped, their spacing was slightly askew, and they didn't seem to be communicating effectively.

In the second quarter, Wade made a defensive adjustment, switching from a man-to-man to a 1–2–2 alignment. The Poets proceeded to outscore the Warriors by a margin of 23–4 in the second quarter. The zone defense, with the long-armed Wingate and Williams taking turns disrupting Walbrook's offense at the top of the key, forced them into 9 turnovers in the second quarter alone. During the last two minutes of the period, Dunbar outscored the Warriors 12–0.

Despite having taken control of the game by halftime, the Poets were subjected to another of Coach Wade's outbursts at intermission. His invective proved effective. With five minutes remaining in the third quarter, the Poets held a 46–21 lead. Bogues continued to push the tempo, and even though Walbrook began to score with greater regularity in the last quarter, Dunbar cruised to a 70–57 victory that was more dominant than the final score suggested.

Tim Dawson was a force on the inside, grabbing 10 rebounds. The majority of his 17 points came on a variety of intense dunks that resulted from his powerful pursuit of offensive rebounds. Reggie Williams scored 23 points and collected 9 rebounds, Wingate added 10 points, and Muggsy also chipped in with 10 points, 7 assists, and his usual accumulation of steals. Reggie Williams praised Dawson for his offensive rebounding in particular.

On Thursday, the Poets traveled to West Baltimore to take on Carver Vocational-Technical High School. Carver was also undefeated, which added an extra element of intrigue to the buildup, and had actually won more games than Dunbar at this early juncture of the season. The game generated plenty of buzz in the city and was billed as a showdown for first place in the Maryland Scholastic Association's "A" Conference. Once again, the boys were greeted by a hostile atmosphere and a packed gymnasium, with folks clamoring to see someone give the Poets a competitive game. They would not get one on that afternoon, though.

The game that everyone was calling a showdown turned out to be a mismatch. The Bears tried a slow-tempo approach, hoping to stop the Dunbar attack. They had a modicum of success, holding the Poets to only 28 points at halftime. But offensively, they struggled mightily against Dunbar's viselike defense, converting only 2 of 16 field goal attempts.

"No team can run with Dunbar and win," Carver coach Bobby Graves told the *Baltimore News-American* after the game. "We just wanted to play with patience and wait for an open shot. Defensively, we did fine. We packed the 2–3 zone and forced Dunbar to shoot from outside. But we couldn't put the ball in the basket in the first half."

Things went from bad to worse for Carver in the second half. Dunbar's smothering defensive pressure forced Carver into 8 turnovers in the third quarter. Dunbar's running attack took off. With Muggsy running a flawless fast break, the Poets jumped out with a 17–2 spurt at the outset of the period. At the end of three quarters, the score was 47–19. The second and third units took advantage of their extended playing time as Dunbar made a deafening statement. In a game that featured two undefeated teams squaring off for first place, the Poets won easily, 74–29.

———

Leon Howard, despite beaming with pride at the performances of his erstwhile charges, kept a low profile whenever he attended Dunbar's games. He made a conscious effort to be inconspicuous. The college recruiters were now starting to pour into Baltimore, hoping to sign some of the city's top players. Howard knew that Bob Wade was leery of Howard's relationships with some of his players and the sway that he could possibly have in the recruiting process. The recruiters, if they were good at their craft, also knew how influential Howard was with the players who had grown up playing for him at the Lafayette Recreation Center.

"Some of the college coaches, I just wasn't comfortable with their recruiting styles," said Wade. "They would try to backdoor the rules and boundaries that I specifically set up to make sure that my guys' best interests were being looked out for. They'd talk to the neighborhood guys, whoever they felt could have an influence on the kid and his family, and they would use that to try to get an upper hand in the recruiting battle. And Leon had a lot of influence with those kids."

Wade didn't want his boys on the phone all night talking to recruiters. He instructed his players to notify him immediately if any of the college coaches violated the parameters that he put in place. If they wanted to call a player's home, Wade gave them specific times that were acceptable. He invited the college coaches to watch the team's practices and allowed them to have conversations with the players in his office, under his supervision.

"I wanted everything done aboveboard. I'd seen too many

guys get burned. These kids needed to enjoy themselves and not get pressured by the recruiting process."

The Lafayette Recreation Center's all-star games now featured actual game uniforms that were supplied by the Runnin' Rebels of the University of Nevada, Las Vegas, and their head coach, Jerry Tarkanian. Leon Howard was able to make a phone call to any number of college coaches and get, strictly on the strength of his word alone, a scholarship opportunity for a lesser-known player. At Howie Garfinkel's prestigious Five-Star camps, Leon Howard spoke with legends like University of North Carolina Head Coach Dean Smith, Maryland's Lefty Driesell, and Louisville's Denny Crum.

"I was not in the business of selling my kids," said Howard. "I loved those kids and my relationships with them, and their families were more important to me than where they were going to play their college ball and what could possibly be in it for me. Coach Wade knew that I was tight with my kids and their families and wasn't sure of my motivations at the time. I knew he didn't want me to be around Dunbar that much, so I'd sneak into the gym from time to time, sit in some far-off seat in the bleachers, and just watch my guys play. I respected how Bob wanted to run his ship."

Wade wasn't impressed by celebrity college coaches or the salesmanship of some of the top assistants who were ubiquitous at the school's games and practices. He didn't care whether his kids made it to the pros. Having been in their shoes a generation earlier, he wanted them to find a school that was going to look after their best interests, get a college degree, and come back to the community with something to offer.

Wade had once been an athletic prodigy from the same East Baltimore streets that his players came from. He wore the same

Dunbar uniform as a teenager. His experiences after high school and college gave him a dogged determination to use sports to build character and provide his kids with the opportunities that had once been afforded him.

Wade was born in East Baltimore on December 9, 1944. His mother, Mattie, cooked and cleaned house—washing, dusting, scrubbing, ironing, and looking after her small apartment as if it were one of those big houses up in Milford where the prominent doctors at Johns Hopkins Hospital lived. Mattie fussed over her two infant children, Bob and his sister, Delores, who was a year older, while her husband Edward put in long hours at the Sparrows Point Bethlehem Steel plant on the city's southern tip in Dundalk. Mattie and Edward had fallen in love and married as teenagers in Buckingham County, Virginia, in a hamlet called Dillwyn. Word about decent union wages to be earned in Baltimore had filtered down there. Eager to escape a future of sharecropping the land that his parents and their parents had, Edward made his way up north. As Baltimore boomed during World War II and steel became king, the many people who relocated from the rural Carolinas and the Virginia Tidewater began to realize the American dream.

Edward Wade was among the more than five million African Americans who departed the farms and fields of the rural South and flooded Baltimore and other northern cities eager for their slice of the American pie. Although he landed in a segregated Baltimore, where the black population was squeezed into a few teeming neighborhoods on the city's east and west sides, Edward had better prospects there than in the racially charged atmosphere in Virginia. Edward sent for his young wife in 1940.

The couple rented a one-bedroom apartment in the 1900 block of East Orleans Street—five blocks from the current Dunbar High School—and started a family.

One day, in 1948 when young Bob was four years old, Mattie waited for Edward to come home from work. He never did. Like so many other cowardly men, he walked out the door never to return, abandoning his family.

Uneducated and with no work experience, Mattie had to take care of two kids on her own. Mattie Wade never asked anybody for a handout. She closed her eyes and prayed, refusing to be trapped by circumstances. Mattie found a job, first as a domestic, and later at S. S. Shapiro and Sons textile factory in the O'Donnell Street industrial park in South Baltimore.

Initially hamstrung to make the monthly rent, she pooled resources with her older brother Linwood and his wife, Edith, who'd previously made their transition from tenant farming in the South to the big city and were raising their own five children in a three-story house in Baltimore. Bob slept in a bed with his mother while his sister shared a bed with two cousins. The other three cousins shared another bed. Mattie would rise before the sun and leave her children's clean, freshly pressed clothes laid out. By the time they woke up, she was hours into her work shift. Bob and Delores would eat their breakfast and make their way to school together.

Young Bob was an excellent student. Education was at the top of his mother's priority list, and the banter around the house with the seven cousins normally centered around a healthy academic competitiveness. Mattie and the kids lived with her brother's family for eight years, scrimping and saving and struggling to make ends meet. Then, combining their meager funds, she and her sister Georgia, who had one son, rented a two-and-a-half-bedroom row house in the same East Baltimore neighborhood that Bob and Delores had known their entire lives. The new living situation was a step up from living with Linwood, his wife, and his five kids. Bob and his cousin Charles shared a bedroom in the Castle Street house, as did Mattie and cousin Georgia, while Delores luxuriated in her own half bedroom.

Bob absorbed Mattie's work ethic, observing that she never complained about the twelve hours a day spent at her job or her daily struggles and responsibilities.

"I learned from her example that if you work hard and treat your fellow man the way you want to be treated, you could make it in life," said Wade.

He also learned from his mother never to incorporate the word *can't* into his vocabulary. She could have easily given up, but she found a way to put food on the table, give her kids a decent home, and make them feel loved and important.

"Coach Wade was relentless, and he would get on all of us," said Keith Wallace. "He was always telling us, yelling at us, especially when we were exhausted and felt like we didn't have anything to give, that we could bend our knees more, that we could run faster, that we could get to the spot in time to trap the ball or take a charge. He would always say, 'The words *I can't* should be taken out of your vocabulary. Take them out! You can do whatever you set your mind to.' "

His players never knew that the messages he screamed about hard work, commitment, and excellence were lessons he'd internalized during his youth.

CHAPTER NINE

"Bogues Is the Real Thing"

DUNBAR'S NEXT GAME, AGAINST Lake Clifton, was on the calendar for Saturday, January 16. But due to another blizzard, it was postponed and rescheduled for the next week. Meanwhile, over that weekend, the Poets were paying attention to a tournament being held in Philadelphia.

Calvert Hall was participating in the Pepsi Challenge Tournament, being played in the Spectrum, the home of the NBA's Philadelphia 76ers. In the championship game, Calvert Hall met New Jersey's Camden High School, a perennial powerhouse. Calvert Hall and Camden were ranked number one and number two in the country. Camden featured a player whom many regarded as the country's top prospect in the senior class, 6-foot-8 forward Billy Thompson, who had already committed to play for Louisville.

"Look, we wanted to get our hands on Calvert Hall; that was no secret," said Bogues. "We knew those guys, they lived in the neighborhood. They got scholarships to go to private school. We were cool, there wasn't any animosity, but once we stepped on the court, it was about competition and pride. And we'd played against them over the summers for years. We knew we were better than them. But we were more interested in that game because we had Camden on our schedule that year; we'd be playing them in about a month. And we had to play them in New Jersey, in their home gym, where they hadn't lost in a long time. That was a huge game that everybody was already getting excited about because some people said that Camden was really the only team left on our schedule that might have a chance to beat us. So we wanted to see what happened when they played Calvert Hall."

For most of the championship game, it looked like Calvert Hall would suffer their first defeat of the year. Camden led 55–50 with 4:30 left in the game, but despite some horrible shooting from the field and the free-throw line for most of the contest, Calvert Hall mounted a furious comeback in the game's waning moments. They eventually won, 67–62.

"When we heard that it had been a close game, that Calvert Hall almost lost, we couldn't wait to get to Camden," said Bogues. "We weren't dismissing any of the teams we had to play before then, though. Coach Wade made sure of that. We respected every team that we played against and didn't overlook anybody, but we wanted that Camden game bad. We felt like we might not get a chance to play Calvert Hall, but if Camden played them close, that was going to be our opportunity to send a message to the rest of the country."

But Muggsy had already sent a message with his early-season play. *Baltimore News-American* writer Bernie Miklasz penned a small item on January 20 with the headline "Bogues Is the Real Thing."

"Everyone knows how good Calvert Hall point guard Pop

Tubman is," wrote Miklasz. "But Pop isn't the only one in town. Over at Dunbar, there's a pretty good one named Tyrone Bogues. Bogues, a junior, is only 5-6 [Muggsy was actually 5 foot 3], but there probably isn't a quicker player or a better defensive guard in the city. With Bogues manning the point, Dunbar has almost perfect chemistry this season and the Poets are playing incredible basketball. In his first game as a Poet, Bogues had 13 steals and 10 assists—while playing in a little more than half the game."

Miklasz wrote a column in the next day's sports section titled "Dunbar Taking the MSA 'A' Conference by Storm." He observed, "Perhaps only a February 13 showdown in New Jersey against highly regarded Camden stands in the way of Dunbar's perfect season."

The talk about a possible unbeaten season, though, did not please Bob Wade.

"Everybody was telling the kids how good they were, and it's easy to lose focus and get a big head when you're a teenager and everybody is patting you on the back, calling you great," said Wade. "I made sure that in practice, they got some medicine to cure any big heads that might have been growing."

"We looked forward to the games so much because, after the way we practiced, the games were like a vacation to us," said Wingate. "Coach wore us out in practice. I mean he worked us like you wouldn't believe."

Despite the expectations, however, the players would sometimes test his limits. One afternoon prior to practice, Muggsy, David Wingate, and Tim Dawson allowed their hunger and innocent mischievousness to get the better of them. They figured that they could skip out on their last-period class and run over to the Old Town Market and grab some cheesesteak sandwiches before study hall. They thought no one would notice—but they didn't realize that nothing happened in the Dunbar neighborhood without Bob Wade knowing about it.

"When we came sneaking in through the back door, Coach Wade was standing right there waiting for us," said Dawson.

Furious, Wade took the trio behind closed doors to get his point across in his unique way.

"Coach was tough on us because he really cared about us," said Bogues. "I think we were all a little hurt because we felt like we had let him down. And he made sure that not only the three of us, but everybody on the team paid the price with some extra running with those bricks after practice."

After easily defeating Poly in their next game to run their record to 15–0, they destroyed Lake Clifton again, 75–42, in the scheduled makeup game. Williams, Graham, Dawson, and Wingate combined to score 65 of the team's overall 75 points. In their next game on Wednesday, January 27, they annihilated Mervo, 94–39. Reggie Williams had another great performance against the Mustangs with 29 points, while Dawson chipped in with 19, and Wingate added 14.

Two days later, at home, they dispatched Walbrook for the second time, 59–42. Once again, the Poets, fueled by their defensive pressure, were led offensively by Williams, who snagged 9 rebounds and connected on 7 of his 11 shot attempts, scoring 16 first-half points en route to his game-high total of 19. Wingate scored 17. In the second half, Walbrook sagged inside and attempted to surround Williams and curtail his early dominance. Recognizing the shift in strategy, the Poets began whizzing the ball to Wingate, who scored 12 points in the final two quarters while converting 8 of his 12 field goal attempts for the game.

"Those two have been phenomenal all season," Wade told the *News-American* after the game. "We usually try to get the ball inside to Russ. But if teams start sagging inside too much, that frees up David outside.

"There were a lot of games where we could have gotten over a hundred points, but I liked to change the pace from time to time and give teams that were scouting us something to think about," said Wade. "Sometimes, we'd go to some isolation plays on the wing for Gary, Reggie, and David, sometimes we'd push, and other times we'd let Muggsy work his magic while dribbling through half-court defenses. We were prepared for any style that an opposing team would try to throw at us."

The day after handily beating Walbrook, the boys were once again sitting on Mr. Parran's bus. Public school students had a three-day weekend while the teachers participated in a professional staff development day on Friday. The team pulled out of Baltimore at 7:00 a.m. en route to Erie, Pennsylvania, where they'd face off against McDowell High School on Saturday evening.

The ride to Erie was a long one, about seven hours, as the bus snaked across Interstate 70 through the slushy remnants of the previous winter storm. During the morning portion of the drive, the cabin was somewhat subdued. But once they stopped near Pittsburgh, at about midway through the trip, to grab a fast-food lunch of greasy burgers and fries, the jokes, music, and laughter amplified.

Wade, looking back from his front row seat, couldn't help but shake his head and laugh at the antics of the guys cracking jokes on one another. But he was in more of a reflective mood due to the geography of the road trip. He spent a good portion of the ride thinking about his own youthful days, his mother, and the influence that athletics had had on his own life journey.

———

As a kid, Wade's Sundays were always spent at Bible study, Sunday school, and listening to the sermons of the Reverend Grant at the Southern Baptist Church on Bond and Preston Streets. In accordance with her strict Christian principles, his mother, Mattie, was very firm with him and his sister, Delores. If she said something needed to be done, it was not up for debate.

"All she had to do was look at you hard, and you got it together real quick," said Wade. "She was very caring, I knew that she worked extremely hard, and she was always there for us, sacrificing everything. I never wanted to disappoint my mother."

He acquired the nickname Cinderfella from the neighborhood kids because of Mattie's tight leash. When he and Delores tried to stretch their curfew a few minutes past the limit, they could hear, amid all the chatter and evening noise on the block, the squeaking of Mattie's bedroom window being raised. They'd break instantly into a sprint toward the front door as their mother poked her head outside. She rarely got past "I thought I told you—" before they came scampering through the vestibule. Mattie was a fixture at PTA meetings, despite her exhausting work schedule, establishing relationships with the teachers and inserting herself into the fabric of the school.

Whatever sport was in season, Wade played on the streets. After school, he'd drop his books at home and run to the nearest field for sandlot baseball and football games. From there, it was on to the basketball court. Sports occupied his time in the afternoon while Mattie was still at work. By the time he got home after a few hours of competition with the neighborhood boys, the scrumptious aromas of Mattie's cooking would greet him at the door. On the weekends, he played from sunup to sundown.

During one sandlot baseball game, Wade was not doing very well playing third base. His friend, Clyde "Yummy" Red, joked that Wade was not looking cool at all, making all those errors. "Man, you're looking real flaky over there," Red is purported to have said, generating a healthy swell of laughter from his buddies. From that day forward, Wade forever became known around the neighborhood by the street nickname Flakie. To this day, it's what his wife and closest friends call him.

Excelling in Dunbar's academically competitive college prep program, Wade became the Poets' starting quarterback during his sophomore year. On the hardwood, he was a serviceable small forward, the team's sixth man. On the baseball diamond, he played every position except pitcher and earned a tryout with the Cincinnati Reds professional baseball team. While others talked about the money he could make playing pro baseball straight out of high school, his mother crushed that pipe dream. "You need to go to school and further your education. I don't want you working in a textile factory like me," she said.

His high school coach and mentor at Dunbar, Sugar Cain, encouraged Wade to attend Baltimore's Morgan State, the historically black college. Cain coached Wade in every sport: football, basketball, and baseball.

Cain was a legendary coach in the region. He cut a dashing figure in the community and on the sidelines, known as much for his regal bearing, handsome features, and sartorial splendor as his basketball coaching acumen. During the early 1940s, Cain was a skinny but rugged 6-foot-3 football and basketball player at Morgan State. He later played briefly with the Harlem Globetrotters, and he eventually earned a master's degree from Columbia University in physical education.

An affable man with infectious humor, he spoke with the eloquence of higher education and could handle any practice drill, humiliating a hotshot player with a swollen head that needed to be humbled. In 1964, a physician advised him to give up coaching due to a worsening ulcer. Cain ignored the advice and elected to have a surgical procedure that removed half of his stomach. In addition to his duties as athletic director, Cain coached basketball at Dunbar for thirty-two years, compiling a record of 485–105. He also led the varsity football and baseball teams. Over the years, he declined countless overtures to enter college coaching.

"He was like my idol, my mentor, the man I latched on to, my surrogate father," said Wade. "My dream was to go to college and major in physical education and be able to coach teams like Mr. Cain. He was the person I wanted to emulate."

Mattie beamed with pride as friends, coworkers, and even her bosses, who'd read of her son's accomplishments in the daily papers' sports sections, offered congratulations. Although she could not see him play due to her work schedule, Mattie religiously cut out his newspaper clippings, kept a scrapbook, and supported him as much as she could.

To earn an extra buck during his junior and senior years in high school, Wade performed landscaping work for Dr. Alan Woods, an eye surgeon at Johns Hopkins for whom his aunt worked as a domestic. He cut the grass, gathered twigs, raked leaves, and stacked piles of wood at the doctor's house in the affluent Milford neighborhood. The president of his graduating class in 1963, Wade was awarded a football scholarship to Morgan State and gave an address at Dunbar's commencement.

"I was an athlete, but I was not a dumb jock," said Wade. "To stand before the student body was a big moment in my life. That was like a carryover value for me when I began coaching, because I would always tell the kids, 'Don't sit in the back of the class; sit in the front. Let the teacher know who you are; let's erase the stereotype of the dumb jock.'"

As a student at Morgan State, Wade entered into a relationship with his next coaching mentor, the legendary Earl C. Banks. Under Banks's stewardship, Morgan sent its fair share of gridiron stars into the pros.

Wade spent his first college season as the third-string quarterback. He ran the scout team in practice, impressing the coaching staff with his agility, composure, leadership, and athleticism. When future Cleveland Brown star and National Football League Hall of Famer Leroy Kelly, who started at halfback and cornerback, suffered a deep thigh bruise toward the end of the season, the defensive coaches convinced Banks to shift Wade to cornerback. In the Bears' last game of the season, against Florida A&M in the Orange Blossom Classic, Wade started at right cornerback. The offensive coaching staff never got to work with him again. He started every game at right cornerback for the next three seasons. Seated in the stands at every home game was the impeccably dressed Sugar Cain. During Wade's sophomore year, Mattie parked herself in the crowded bleachers of Morgan's football stadium, staring wide-eyed at her son. It was the first time she ever saw him play in person.

At 6 foot 3, 215 pounds, Wade was a large, ball-hawking defensive back, covering vast stretches of real estate in the secondary. His bone-crushing tackles deflated opponents. The scouts from the AFL took notice of his size, mastery of the fundamentals, and ability to pancake ball carriers. During his junior season, the pros began compiling a dossier on him. On July 16, 1966, before his final college season, he married his college sweetheart, Carolyn Edwards, in a small ceremony at St. Rita's Catholic Church in Dundalk, Maryland.

"She wasn't pregnant and there wasn't any shotgun. We were in love," he said.

In 1965, the Kansas City Chiefs of the American Football League drafted a 6-foot-5 wide receiver out of Prairie View A&M University named Otis Taylor. Taylor possessed height and speed that redefined the position in the professional ranks. In 1966, he ran roughshod over the smaller, overmatched defensive backs who attempted to cover him, accumulating a franchise record 1,297 receiving yards. At the end of the season, on January 15, 1967, one of the most pivotal days in the history of American professional sports, Taylor and his Kansas City Chiefs played in the first AFL–NFL World Championship Game (later renamed the Super Bowl), losing to Vince Lombardi's powerful Green Bay Packers in front of sixty million television viewers. As a result of Otis Taylor's significance to Kansas City's offense, pro personnel directors began scouring the collegiate ranks for tall, strong, fast defensive backs to deal with this new breed of wide receiver.

Relaxing in his mother-in-law's house in the Turner's Station neighborhood, where he and Carolyn lived for their first year of marriage, Wade watched the news one night, months shy of receiving his bachelor's degree in physical education, as Channel 11 sportscaster Vince Bagley announced that Bubba Smith, the ferocious defensive lineman out of Michigan State, had been the overall number one pick in the NFL draft. Willie Lanier, Wade's teammate at Morgan, was chosen by the Chiefs in the second round. Before signing off, Bagley uttered the words that made Wade almost fall out of the bed—"and in the fifteenth round, the Baltimore Colts selected Robert Wade, defensive back out of Morgan State."

Wade received a contract for $15,000.

"I'm rich," he whispered to himself as he signed the document.

Although he was a late-round draft pick, Wade and another rookie, Preston Pearson, impressed Coach Don Shula and the Colts' staff. In training camp at Westminster College (now McDaniel College), Wade's idol, Lenny Moore, the Colts' superstar running back, took a liking to him.

"Lenny told me all about the things to look out for and the overall importance of guarding your life from the pitfalls that he'd seen guys fall prey to," said Wade. "To this day, we're very close. He was my mentor as an athlete and an individual."

Happier than a kid in a candy store with a pocketful of money, Wade could not believe that he was sharing a locker room with guys whose pictures he'd cut out of magazines and taped to his wall just a few years earlier. He'd walk by the stall of Johnny Unitas and pause for a moment, smiling and shaking his head. In practice, although the game was much faster than what he was accustomed to in college, his mastery of the fundamentals and attention to technique served him well while covering wide receivers Raymond Berry and Wally Richardson. The Colts had to put Wade on waivers because of their depth in the secondary even though defensive backfield coach Chuck Noll wanted to keep him on the roster. The Washington Redskins were in hot pursuit when Wade's name hit the waiver wire, unbeknownst to him. Otto Graham, then the Redskins' head coach, called Coach Banks at Morgan, who looked all over town for Wade, to no avail. The Colts had stashed him where no one could reach him, and once he cleared waivers, signed him to the team's practice squad.

His rookie year, although he didn't appear in any games, he went head-to-head with the formidable Colts offense of Unitas, Berry, and Moore. During the 1967–68 season, the team went 11–1–2, but missed the four-team playoffs after losing to the Los Angeles Rams in the divisional tiebreaker.

Wade was traded to the Pittsburgh Steelers the very next season, became a starter, and finished as the runner-up to the Atlanta Falcons' Claude Humphrey as the NFL's Defensive Rookie of the Year. In Pittsburgh, Wade lived in the Washington Plaza apartments, across from the city's downtown Civic Arena, with other players who didn't own homes in the area. His apartment was a short, three-block walk to Pitt Stadium, where the Steelers played their home games.

Before players entered the stadium, in the area around the players' entrance, a number of fans gathered to greet them. Whenever Wade walked into the stadium on game days, he was always spoken to by the same older man, who gathered along with the other rabid fans.

"Hi, Bob Wade. How ya doin'?"

Wade would return the man's greeting as he briskly made his entrance. "I'm fine, thanks. How you doin'?"

At the end of his first season in Pittsburgh, Wade felt that his onfield performance warranted a pay raise. He held out for a better contract and was rebuffed by a young Dan Rooney, who was negotiating on behalf of his father, the team's owner, Art Rooney. "Sign this or somebody else will," Rooney told Wade point-blank. Wade conferred with Coach Banks at Morgan State. Earl Banks taught his boys to be men and stand firm if they were in the right. Wade did, but he was traded to the Washington Redskins.

Vince Lombardi, the standard against which all football coaches are measured, had taken on the challenge of leading the Redskins after winning the first two Super Bowls with the Green Bay Packers. Lombardi believed in simplicity. His teams did not run complex plays, but those they did run they drilled incessantly. But the old NFL films of Vince Lombardi do not show the entire man. He was, indeed, a strict disciplinarian with a fierce competitive desire to win. But he was also intensely wedded to the concept of family.

"Lombardi always said that the three most important things in our lives were God, family, and the team, in that order," said Wade. "The players were allowed to bring their kids to practices on Saturdays, and Lombardi would officiate the games that the kids would play. His wife traveled with him at all times. If you had an emergency and it was family-related, he gave you time off to take care of your family."

Wade internalized Lombardi's attention to detail and how, at practices, the team ran their simple plays over and over and over again until they were mastered. It mattered not that the other team knew what Lombardi's players were going to run; what mattered was their inability to stop what everyone knew was coming.

After the 1970 season with the Redskins, Wade experienced another change of scenery. Traded to the Denver Broncos, he earned a starting job in the secondary before suffering a severe hand injury. He had surgery on a shattered wrist and was left, for all practical purposes, with the use of one good hand. As a defensive back, this proved a tremendous liability. Although Wade had been named to the NFL's All-Rookie team two years earlier, his playing days were over. He hung up his cleats and came back home. Having already obtained his teaching license and certification, he began working for the Baltimore City Public Schools as a middle school teacher. Wade extracted important elements from all of his coaches and mentors, but his coaching philosophies directly mirrored those of Lombardi.

"At Dunbar, we ran the same offensive set against any defense," Wade said. "The press break was the same as the half-court offense. It was all about execution and simplicity. We practiced and practiced and practiced until the players didn't have to think. We practiced everything from our offense and defense down to our pregame drills until it all became second nature."

Shortly after Wade walked away from professional football, Mattie got word that Edward, the husband who had walked out on her in 1948, had died. Apparently, he'd gone to live in Pittsburgh, finding work in that city's bustling steel industry. After talking with Bob and Delores, they decided to attend Edward's services.

Walking into the funeral home, Wade approached the casket and looked at the man lying inside. He didn't have much recollection of his father, as Edward had left when he was only four years old. But scanning the dead man's face, Wade sensed a vague familiarity with him. He felt as if he'd seen and spoken to this man before. And then it hit him.

"Hi, Bob Wade. How ya doin'?"

Wade was looking at his father, the man who had waited with the crazy Steelers fans in front of the players' entrance to Pitt Stadium, the man who had spoken to him before every home game.

"I thought he was just a fan," said Wade.

Wade's father lived in the ghetto known as "the Hill," within walking distance of his son's downtown apartment. But Edward Wade couldn't find the nerve to tell Bob who he was. Wade approached the mortician and instructed him to remove the man from the cheap casket. He paid, on the spot, for a decent one.

"Why are you doing that? You're gonna do that for him?" Mattie asked, confused.

"He's my father," Wade softly replied.

The majority of the players he coached at Dunbar High School did not have their fathers in their lives. Although stern and tough and abrasive at times, Wade was close with all of his boys. Like his own coaches, he was the father to the boys of Dunbar that he himself had never had.

———

As Mr. Parran steered his bus into the parking lot of the team's motel in Erie, Wade and Lynn Badham looked at each other and smiled without exchanging words.

"I was just happy, after what happened in New York, that we'd be staying in a decent place," said Wade. "The folks in Erie had invited us up there, and they were known for having one of the toughest high school basketball teams in the region. This game looked like it would be a good test for us, especially with venturing into another hostile environment. As the season unfolded, we knew that the Erie trip was going to help prepare us for the game against Camden, which was coming up soon."

From the moment that Dunbar accepted the invitation to play the game in Erie, the communication between both of the schools' contingents had been very cordial and friendly. When the busload of Poet Followers arrived in northwestern Pennsylvania, the locals welcomed them and invited them out for a festive evening of eating, drinking, and partying.

After running into the lobby to get everyone's room keys, Wade stepped back onto the bus to break down the rest of the day's itinerary.

"Go up to your rooms, change into your practice gear, and I want everyone back on this bus in fifteen minutes," the coach told his players. "We're going to head over to the gym and do a quick walk-through of the game plan. After we practice, we'll come back here and you guys can shower and change back into your collared shirts and ties. Our hosts have made arrangements for us to go out to dinner at a local restaurant tonight. I know we've been on this bus for eight hours and it's already been a long day. So after dinner, we'll just come back to the hotel and get a good night's rest. This is a very tough team that we came up here to play, fellas. That gym is going to be packed tomorrow.

We're one of the top-ranked teams in the country and, year in and year out, McDowell is one of the best teams around. They are going to be ready to fight and give us everything we want. I'm excited to play this game. Let's have some fun, enjoy this weekend, and kick their ass tomorrow. See you guys in fifteen minutes."

After the brief practice and a hearty dinner, the boys were back in their rooms, watching television. Marshall Goodwin was charged with ensuring that nothing was amiss after curfew.

"I was walking up and down the corridors, making sure the guys were where they were supposed to be," said Goodwin. "The guys seemed pretty relaxed. I didn't see any girls or any partying or anything like that going on. Plus, it was freezing cold up there, so if the guys weren't in their own rooms, they were just hanging out in some of the other guys' rooms. The rooms were pretty spread out, so after making sure that everybody was in their own rooms by curfew, I felt pretty confident that there wouldn't be any problems."

But while Goodwin was convinced that the guys were resting comfortably, a restless David Wingate hatched a plan, along with the Wallace brothers, for some harmless fun.

"I got ahold of a bucket from one of the maintenance closets and decided to fill it up with some water," said Wingate. "We decided that we'd go knocking on the other guys' doors and once they opened it, I'd run in there, throw the water, and then we'd just run out. It was silly. And we couldn't stop laughing, thinking about it."

The first door they knocked on belonged to Tim Dawson and his brother Ellis. When one of the Dawson brothers grudgingly got out of bed and opened the door, Wingate rushed in with the exuberance of an invading army. He took a few steps, reared back and, in one swift underhanded motion, sent the entire contents of the bucket into the air. The water crashed onto the television, which the brothers had been watching.

"Man, the TV damn near exploded," said Wingate. "Sparks came flying out of it, and there was smoke everywhere. I thought it might blow up and start a fire. I ran out of there so fast. I was laughing, but I was scared, too. I knew that if Mr. Wade found out, he might kill us. So we didn't say anything, even to the other guys on the team."

When Wade walked up to Wingate during breakfast the next day and said, "Hey, David," Wingate almost confessed on the spot.

"We were all scared of Coach because we knew that he didn't play around," said Wingate. "He always stressed, especially when we went out of town, that we represent ourselves, our families, and our school with dignity and class. And when he looked at me the next morning, my guilty conscience had me convinced that he knew about the TV. He knew everything, like if we cut class, if we were having problems with teachers, if we were hanging out with people that we shouldn't have been around. He knew all that stuff; nothing got by him. I was scared, but I didn't say anything. I thought if we could get back to Baltimore without him finding out, that it would all blow over."

Wingate and the Dawson brothers were walking on eggshells for the entire day, but felt relieved when they boarded the bus to head over to their game that evening.

McDowell was a large school, with more than two thousand students. Athletically, the Trojans were well known for their football program. The area itself, with Cleveland and Pittsburgh nearby, drew much of its pride from football. Their hoops team might not have had players being recruited by college basketball powerhouses, but they were stocked with strong, fast, and agile athletes who excelled in the rugged gridiron game.

"Those guys were big and strong," said Bogues. "I remember Coach telling us that it was going to be a physical game, because they had a couple of guys who were really good football players who were supposed to be going to play at Pitt or Penn State. We felt like this was going to be a good challenge, and we were excited to take the court against them."

The town was equally excited. The gymnasium was standing room only. The excited feelings continued during the introduction of both teams, as the Dunbar players presented their counterparts at McDowell with City of Baltimore key chains as a goodwill gesture, promising to treat them with reciprocal warmness if the Trojans wanted to travel to Baltimore for another matchup in the future.

At the outset of the game, both teams seemed to be feeling each other out like heavyweight boxers in the opening round of a championship bout. Halfway through the first quarter, Dunbar led 8–7 as the roars and yells from the McDowell fans suggested that they believed they could pull off the upset. The Trojans walked into the game having won ten straight. They seemed confident that they could extend their winning streak until Dunbar turned up the defensive heat. The Poets' lead quickly mushroomed into a 16–7 advantage at the end of the first period.

McDowell still looked to be within striking distance early in the second quarter, trailing 20–11. But Reggie Williams began to assert himself, scoring 8 straight points. With Muggsy running the well-oiled fast break and the Poets' defense suffocating the Trojan offense, the game's outcome soon became apparent. Before the teams jogged to their respective locker rooms at halftime with the visitors leading, 28–13, the Dunbar victory was all but assured. The only question was how bad the visitors would beat up on their gracious hosts.

With Muggsy delighting the crowd with his steals, speed, and passing, Williams, Wingate, and Dawson putting on yet another open-court slam-dunk exhibition, and Gary Graham augmenting his defensive prowess with his midrange and long-distance jump shots, Dunbar put the game out of reach early in the third quarter. Leading 35–20, they went on one of their patented offensive spurts, scoring 12 unanswered points to stretch the lead to 47–20. McDowell fought valiantly to close the third period, yet they still trailed 51–28.

When the lead reached 34 points with four minutes left in the game, as his team was in the midst of a torrid shooting stretch, connecting on 16 of their 21 second-half shot attempts, Wade emptied his bench. The Trojans continued to fight, scoring 19 points in the fourth quarter. Their high-scoring output in the fourth quarter irked Wade, who was not pleased with the defensive efforts of his subs. He was certain to address that displeasure in the team's next practice. But overall, he was satisfied that, even with the porous defense of the game's final minutes, Dunbar's swarming pressure had forced McDowell to miss 30 of their 44 shot attempts. Williams led the Poets with 20 points, as Graham and Wingate added 18 and 14 points respectively. Muggsy scored 8, but it was his overall floor generalship that garnered the heaviest applause.

Throughout the game, Wade was receiving weather updates from Parran. A storm was moving in.

"We were scheduled to spend the night in Pennsylvania after the game," said Wade. "The game didn't start until seven o'clock in the evening and when we planned the trip, we figured that we'd go back to the hotel after the game, get some sleep, and then head back to Baltimore on Sunday morning. But with the amount of snowfall that they were predicting, the chances of us being stranded in Erie for a few days became a scenario that we had to take into consideration. So we all had one eye on the game and the other on the approaching storm."

In the relaxed and happy visitors' locker room after the game, Wade gathered his boys.

"With the exception of the final few minutes, our defensive effort tonight was outstanding," the coach said. "Our starting unit played a great game. But we'll be doing some extra running on Monday due to what I saw defensively from our second and third units. Other than that, I'm happy with how you guys carried yourselves on this trip. Now, this storm is moving in and it's about to get ugly. We've decided that instead of spending the night here, we're gonna go back to the hotel, grab our things, check out, and get on the road so we're not stuck here."

After running back to the hotel and swiftly packing their bags, the boys were back on the bus, inching through the falling snow and toward the highway en route back to East Baltimore. The Poet Followers decided to spend another night hanging out in Erie with their newfound friends. As the boys left Erie behind, David Wingate was in jovial spirits, even more than his usual cheerful disposition. The more distant that Erie appeared in the rearview mirror, the wider his grin became.

"I was just glad that Coach didn't find out about that TV," said Wingate.

The old Greyhound bus crawled down Interstate 79 and through the Pennsylvania Turnpike as the falling snow accumulated around them, en route to Interstate 70, as the boys slept. It took nine hours for Mr. Parran to navigate back home, but they arrived safely.

"That was a great trip, guys," said Wade as he stood at the head of the bus, after Goodwin walked through the cabin and woke the boys up. "We're coming down to the home stretch and have some big games coming up in the next few weeks before we get ready for the playoffs. Get some rest today, your bodies need it. I'll see you in the gym after school tomorrow."

CHAPTER TEN

"Make Baltimore Proud"

AS WADE SAT IN his office on Monday morning, he began making practice preparations for the next few weeks. The Poets were entering the final month of the season. They would have three practices during the current week before games on Thursday and Friday. They would then have a full week to prepare for their game against New Jersey's Camden High School before coming back home to finish the conference season and prepare for the city public school tournament. In addition to the normal practices, Wade also scheduled another set of sessions specifically for college coaches to observe, which he'd done periodically throughout the season.

He felt that there was a lot to be accomplished in the days ahead, in terms of not only winning basketball games, but also getting his seniors more prepared to move toward making their college decisions. With the college coaches in the gym to watch the team work out, he stressed to the younger players that while the University of North Carolina's Dean Smith or Georgetown's

John Thompson might have been there to recruit the highly re-garded players, there would also be an opportunity for them to make a lasting impression.

"Coach Wade always told me that I would have an oppor-tunity to be seen and evaluated by the top college programs," said Bogues. "If I was playing at another school, I think I would have just been seen as another good, short guard from the city. But when those coaches were coming in there to watch Wingate, Gary Graham, Tim Dawson, Reggie Williams, and the other guys on our team, Mr. Wade made sure that those coaches saw how unique I was and that, despite my size, I could play with any-body. He was an advocate for me. There were a lot of coaches from those big-time schools who just didn't believe that a 5-foot-3 guard could play and make an impact on the college level. And to be honest, he couldn't convince some of them to really con-sider me. But there were some coaches who listened to him and watched me more closely not only because of how I played, but because he believed so much in my ability."

After one practice where the college coaches were present, North Carolina's Dean Smith asked Wade if he could sit with some of the players privately in his office. He requested to meet with Tim Dawson, Reggie Williams, and David Wingate.

Dawson said, "We were sitting there in Coach Wade's office with the great Dean Smith and as he started talking, I interrupted him and said, 'Hey, Coach Smith, shouldn't Muggsy be in here as well?' I mean, Muggsy was the best player on our team. And I'll never forget Dean Smith saying that he thought Muggsy was a terrific high school player, but that he wasn't good enough or big enough to play basketball in the ACC."

"The college coaches said that all the time about Muggsy, which I couldn't understand," said Reggie Williams. "We all knew how good he was, but the main thing that all of them said was that he wouldn't be able to play at the next level. Coach Wade was telling Dean Smith, John Thompson, and any other coach who would listen that they needed to recruit Muggsy. Not many of those coaches listened to him."

"When the college coaches were in the gym, it was like a highlight show," said Wingate. "We'd be showing off how fast we could run, how high we could jump, how well we could shoot, just dunking the ball everywhere. But once they left, Coach Wade would get those bricks out, and he'd be yelling and screaming all over again, acting like we were the worst team in Baltimore."

As Wade sat at his desk that Monday morning, jotting down some notes, he reminded himself that the upcoming game against the Patterson High School Clippers would hold some emotional importance for Reggie Lewis. He would be playing with a chip on his shoulder because he'd been cut from the Patterson team the year before. Wade knew that his team would not encounter many problems from the Clippers and figured that he would have an opportunity to get the second and third teams some extended playing time, with hopes that they could correct some of the lackadaisical effort that they showed in Erie.

But his planning was interrupted when the phone rang in his office. After he hung up the phone a few minutes later, he was incensed.

Wade had just learned from the Erie hotel manager about the incident that resulted in the ruined television.

"Coach was so pissed off when he got that phone call from the hotel," said Goodwin. "And the first person that he called and cursed out was me. He was screaming, 'Marshall, your job is to make sure that everyone is in their room and that there is no nonsense going on! You told me that everything was fine when we were up there. I want to know what the hell was going on, and I'm going to get to the bottom of this.' He called me every curse word in the book. He was hot! Coach was very protective of the reputation of Dunbar and those kids. And anything that made it seem like they were a bunch of knuckleheads, like they were a bunch of rowdy city kids from the projects who didn't know how to behave themselves, really left a bad taste in his mouth."

During the school day, Wade was fuming. When he saw Tim and Ellis Dawson walking through the gym in between classes, he marched out of his office and summoned them inside.

"I closed the door, sat them down, and interrogated them," said Wade. "They offered no resistance and gave everybody up. They let me know who was in the room and what happened."

After excusing the Dawson brothers, Wade sat patiently in his office and waited for practice to begin. As the guys began warming up in the gym, shooting around and working individually on their skills, Wingate walked in, grinning from ear to ear. Wade blew his whistle and had everyone gather at half-court. When he mentioned to the team that he'd received a phone call from the hotel in Erie, he stared at the furtive Wingate.

"David had an innocent smile, but he could be very cunning and crafty," said Wade. "He tried to give me that innocent look when I confronted him. And he tried to look baffled, like, 'Who? Me?' He tried to lie his way out of it and persuade me that it had to be somebody else. I took him in my office, alone, and he eventually admitted what he did. A little pressure brought out everything."

Wade was genuinely upset, stressing to Wingate that if word leaked out that he was some type of troublemaker, some college coaches might not offer him a scholarship. He also stressed that

Wingate's silly and immature behavior could possibly ruin opportunities down the road for Dunbar players. Wade reasoned that
if it became known that the Poets were at an out-of-town hotel,
destroying property, some would jump to false conclusions that
the kids in his program were uncontrollable. He pointed out that
sponsors and promoters could stop inviting Dunbar to compete
in those elite out-of-town events. The coach heatedly stressed that
they'd worked too hard to gain recognition on a national level because of the excellence of their basketball program for their reputation to be ruined over a dumb prank. With his hands clenching
Wingate's practice jersey, he forcefully reiterated that a Dunbar
Poet was expected to carry himself in a first-class manner off
the court, at all times. He yanked his star senior back and forth,
reminding him that he didn't want to throw away an opportunity
to go to a great college and one day be able to help his mother.
He lectured, over and again, that succeeding in life was all about
making the correct choices.

After three days of tough practices, the Poets were relieved to
play the Patterson High School Clippers on Thursday, February
4. Throughout the week, Reggie Lewis seemed to be competing
with more focus and determination. The Patterson game was very
important to him, not only because he'd been cut from their team
the year before, but because his brother was the star player there.

"There was definitely some added incentive for Truck during
that week, and Coach made sure that he received a lot of playing time in that game," said Bogues. "We knew that it was an
important game to him."

Patterson didn't stand a chance. Dunbar obliterated them
109–36. Defensively, their execution was flawless. They allowed
the Clippers to score only 11, 7, 10, and 8 points, respectively,
during each quarter. On the offensive end, their transition game

operated at its maximum efficiency as Patterson collapsed under a monsoon of layups, jump shots, and intimidating slam dunks.

David Wingate, eager to put the hotel incident behind him, led the Poets with 20 points, while Reggie Williams added 17, and Gary Graham chipped in with 15. Reggie Lewis had his best game of the season. In addition to his numerous blocked shots and rebounds, he also scored 15 points, a season high for him. When the final buzzer sounded, no one in the gym had a bigger smile than the skinny, 6-foot-5 sub, Truck.

"I just wanted to prove a point to the coach who had cut him," said Wade. "I wanted him to know that the kid could really play. Truck was hurt for a long time after he got cut from the Patterson team because he really wanted to play with his brother Irvin. That was his dream growing up, to start on the same high school team with Irvin. When the guy cut him, he told him that he wasn't good enough to play high school ball. And I just thought that that was preposterous. So I wanted to show Patterson that they made a mistake. And in the case of Truck, their mistake was our gain. We played him more minutes than he normally played in that game, and he definitely answered the call."

The Poets were again in action on the next day, hosting Carver Vocational-Technical High School for their second matchup of the season. Having already clinched first place in the MSA "A" Conference Division I race with their annihilation of Patterson, they showed no signs of complacency and steamrolled the Bears, 88–50. At the end of the first quarter, Carver trailed by only 3 points. But the mirage of a competitive game quickly evaporated.

As usual, Reggie Williams and David Wingate scored the most points, but Gary Graham had a respectable 17 in the game.

"Muggsy, Russ, and Gate got most of the attention, and deservedly so, because they were phenomenal players," said Wade.

"But Gary was just as much of a great player as those guys. He was the unsung hero on the team. He had an incredible work ethic and an advanced understanding of the nuances and geometry of the game. He was an elite, and I mean *elite*, defensive player who took great pride in his effort. He could shoot the ball extremely well, was strong, understood passing angles, sacrificed his own personal statistics for the benefit of his teammates, and was just a bulldog every time he stepped on the court."

———

Anyone who followed Baltimore's basketball scene was interested in watching Gary Graham. In addition to his talent and his skill set, which might have been lost on the casual fan because of the brilliance of Muggsy, Reggie Williams, and David Wingate, Graham's surname carried immense weight in the city's high school basketball world.

All his brothers were excellent players, but his brother Ernie is still mentioned among the city's greatest players ever. The Graham brothers grew up in the rugged North Avenue/Greenmount Avenue corridor. Their father worked at Sparrows Point, the behemoth Bethlehem Steel complex that stretched four miles from end to end and was once a symbol of America's manufacturing superiority. The work was beyond backbreaking and dangerous. It could also be deadly.

Graham's dad also drove a cab in his spare time, and their mom worked as a nurse.

"They worked very hard to try to provide for us and grab their little slice of the American Dream," said Ernie Graham.

The Grahams were firsthand witnesses to the violence and riots that engulfed their East Baltimore community in the wake of Dr. Martin Luther King's assassination in 1968. With the residents unleashing their frustrations at King's death, along with pervasive unemployment, overcrowded housing, and debilitating poverty, the community was obliterated. Throughout the city, over five thousand people were arrested. More than one thousand businesses were destroyed. More than seven hundred people were injured. Six people were killed.

"There was so much tension in the air, and I saw my neighborhood getting burned down to the ground," said Ernie. "There were a lot of businesses on Greenmount Avenue that were looted and set on fire. I remember seeing the army tanks and trucks and military everywhere. I remember people running through the streets and the alleys with televisions and clothes. I remember the smoke and the fire, the gunshots and the constant noise of ambulances."

Ernie's story was much like Skip Wise's: a phenomenal basketball talent that never reached its full potential due to drugs. Away from the basketball court, where he set a University of Maryland record when he dropped 44 points against North Carolina State as a sophomore, he graduated from marijuana, which he began smoking at the age of thirteen, and started dabbling with cocaine.

After he was drafted by the Philadelphia 76ers in the 1981 NBA draft, it became apparent during training camp that his drug use was spiraling out of control. Despite being impressive on the court, he was the last player cut before the season started. He excelled in the Continental Basketball Association and while playing pro ball overseas, but he blew his later tryouts with the Indiana Pacers and the Boston Celtics.

"I was drugged out of my mind," said Ernie.

Drug dealers in Baltimore, and in several other countries as well, were angrily in search of him due to unpaid debts. He estimates that over the course of his pro career overseas, he easily spent over a million dollars on narcotics. He stole from anyone and was a constant presence at pawnshops. His daily life became a nightmare of pain made worse by the sinister and debilitating crack, heroin, and powder cocaine that coursed through his veins.

Gary Graham's brothers had taught him, since the day he began playing, that there were many ways that a good player could impact a game, that he could elevate his team while concentrating on things other than scoring. Casual fans could see Tim Dawson blocking shots and ripping down the rim after getting his offensive rebounds. It was also apparent how fluid, graceful, and skilled Reggie Williams and David Wingate were. And even if one knew absolutely nothing about basketball, he only had to watch Muggsy Bogues for a few minutes to walk away with the understanding of how uniquely talented he was. But with Graham, an individual truly had to understand the nuances and intricacies of the sport in order to accurately gauge his skills and appreciate how significant he was to the team. In the newspapers and on the nightly newscasts, Graham didn't get the credit or the level of attention that the others received. But his coaches, teammates, competitors, opposing coaches, the college recruiters, and true students of the game who followed prep basketball in Baltimore knew how magnificent he truly was.

"Gary brought so much to the team," said Reggie Williams. "He always guarded the other team's best offensive player. And he would just be so physical with them and not allow them to score. He made all the right passes, hit timely shots, and played with a passion every time he was on the court."

————

Dunbar's matchup with Camden was a week away. Without any games until then, Wade was able to focus in on a game plan designed specifically for the Panthers. He felt that his team had been playing exceptionally over their last few games. They'd improved significantly since the beginning of the season. He liked their cohesion, how they competed and motivated one another, and he felt like they were hitting their stride at the optimal time.

The day after the Carver victory, he piled into his friend Woody Williams's car, along with Marshall Goodwin and Edgar Lee Bell, his own former youth league coach and mentor, who had coached Muggsy and Reggie Williams at the Lafayette Rec Center when they were kids. They drove to New Jersey to get a close look at Camden's players.

"Woody was my good friend, and he was an excellent coach," said Wade. "When we played against his Lake Clifton teams, they were always very well drilled. Despite being competitors during the season, we had a great relationship and a lot of mutual respect. He was originally from South Jersey, and he knew the terrain up there, so he volunteered to drive us up to Camden so we could scout them. Mr. Lee, or Tweety Bird as the kids called him, and Marshall both knew the game very well, and I thought we'd have four educated perspectives to bounce off one another as we prepared a strategic plan for that game. So we took a road trip to watch them play against another school in Camden, their local rival, Woodrow Wilson High School."

When the group arrived at Woodrow Wilson, they noticed that Lefty Driesell, the head coach at the University of Maryland, was also in the gym. Driesell was hoping to get Camden's 6-foot-8 power forward Billy Thompson to accept his scholarship offer and become a Terrapin. Thompson was touted by many recruiting analysts as the best high school player in the country who had the potential to be an NBA star one day. Lefty was also in hot pursuit of Wingate. If he could sign those two players, Lefty could reasonably expect to compete for multiple national championships in the near future, something he'd hoped to do when, at his introductory press conference in 1969, he boldly proclaimed that Maryland had the potential to be "the UCLA of the East."

Driesell had had some success at Maryland during the first twelve years of his tenure, with two of his teams advancing as far as the NCAA Tournament's Elite Eight. But that was the closest he'd ever gotten to a national title. His teams had yet to win an Atlantic Coast Conference championship and by February of 1982, he was in the midst of coaching a team that would limp to a 16–13 record while winning only five conference games. Lefty was known as a great recruiter who had turned the moribund program at Davidson College into a national power. But his cupboard in College Park, Maryland, was getting bare. He desperately needed some elite players. He'd long said that he wanted the area's best players to come to Maryland. And he'd been a constant presence at Dunbar High School games for years.

But there was an uneasy and fragile nature to Wade's relationship with Driesell. Ernie Graham, Gary's older brother, had clashed with Driesell during his stay in College Park, and Wade had often been on the receiving end of phone calls from Ernie while he struggled at Maryland. Wade encouraged him to work hard and persevere, as he did with a lot of his former players who called from college to say that they were having some tough times.

There was one particular incident earlier in the season that upset Wade. "After games, our team rule was that every player was to go immediately down to the locker room. Sometimes, fans would spill out onto the court, and things could get crazy, and I just wanted to ensure the safety of my players. After one game, Lefty came on the court to talk to Wingate. I told David that he could talk to him later and to get on down to the locker room.

Lefty was holding David's arm and wouldn't let him go. I raised my voice and told David again to get on down to the locker room, and Lefty and I exchanged some words. I just told him to respect my rules, that was all there was to it. But some people blew it out of proportion, saying I threatened him by saying I wouldn't send another player to Maryland. But that wasn't the case. I never said anything like that to him. If one of my kids wanted to go there and it was a good fit, if that was the decision that they made, I was in support of them going there."

Wade, Goodwin, Bell, and Williams said hello to Driesell and then settled into their seats to scout the Camden Panthers. After the game, they all agreed that Camden was very talented. Wade also thought that they were extremely cocky, especially Billy Thompson. They talked about how Camden ran a lot of their offense through their two star players, Thompson and Kevin Walls, ranked as one of the top point guards in the nation. They agreed that Camden could be vulnerable because they scarcely depended on any set plays while favoring a freer, undisciplined style. Dunbar was going to concede some size, but they felt that the Panthers could not match the Poets in quickness.

"I assumed that Walls would underestimate Muggsy and think that he could take advantage of him because of their height differentials," said Wade. "And the worst thing that anybody who was playing against Muggsy could do was underestimate him. Russ, Gate, Gary, and Muggs were all incredible defensive players. And with Tim holding things down in the paint to block shots and challenge anybody that tried to attack the basket if we had some defensive breakdowns, I thought we had a lot of advantages. I had every bit of faith in our defensive ability, so I liked our chances."

Throughout the week of practice, Wade emphasized the defensive rotations and the players' covering for one another to negate any driving lanes. He felt that if Camden couldn't freelance and was forced to depend on running set plays for the majority of the game, they would be out of their element and unable to make the necessary adjustments.

"Cutting off the baseline and erasing any driving lanes to the basket, that was what we worked on leading into the Camden game," said Wade.

"We knew that Camden liked to run, and we felt like there was not one team in the country that could play the running game better than we could," said Bogues. "We were going to dictate the action. We forced teams to turn the ball over; we knew how to manage and take control of a game. There was a lot of excitement and anticipation during that week leading up to the Camden trip. And Coach basically kept it simple and said that we were going to do what we always did."

With Camden having finished the prior season as the country's number two ranked team, and with their narrow defeat by Calvert Hall earlier in the year, the upcoming game took on a national significance. For high school hoops aficionados in Baltimore, it reminded them of the great 1973 game when Skip Wise and Coach Sugar Cain led Dunbar in an upset against Adrian Dantley and Coach Morgan Wootten's DeMatha team at the downtown Civic Center.

"People all over the city were talking about the Camden game during the week," said Eric Green. "I would be walking down the street wearing my Dunbar basketball jacket, it would be snowing, and people would pull their cars over, sliding all over the ice, and tell me how proud they were of us, how they were rooting for us, and to go out there and make Baltimore proud. There were always rivalries within the city. But for that game, we weren't just playing for Dunbar. We had the whole city behind us, supporting us. It was a pretty big deal. We knew that the national magazines had Billy Thompson ranked as the number one player in America. And we knew that Kevin Walls was considered one of the best point guards. We were really looking forward to that challenge."

The Camden game was also a barometer for a possible matchup against Calvert Hall. That was a game that every basketball fan in the city wanted to see. Many of Dunbar's supporters, along with those whose loyalties belonged to Baltimore's public schools, felt that Calvert Hall was refusing to schedule the game out of fear that the Poets could beat them handily, ruining their undefeated season and a chance at the mythical high school national championship. But Calvert's coach, Mark Amatucci, insisted that a matchup with Dunbar would have to wait. He told the *News-American*'s high school sports columnist Bernie Miklasz, "Right now, we're interested in just two things—winning the Catholic League and winning the Alhambra Tournament. That's all we care about. If we were to play Dunbar, we would only play after the Alhambra Tournament. We're very firm about that."

The problem with that scenario was that the prestigious Alhambra Tournament, held at Frostburg State University in Cumberland, Maryland, and which featured the top eight Catholic high school teams in the country, was played annually during the third weekend in March. This meant that a possible game against Dunbar would have to wait until the end of March. With Dunbar expected to be competing for the Maryland Scholastic Association "A" Conference Championship at the Baltimore Civic Center to conclude its season, barring a major upset, Dunbar's season was likely to end on Sunday, February 28. This meant that Dunbar would be inactive for four weeks before playing Calvert.

"It's unreasonable to expect any team to go a month in between games and play well," Wade told Miklasz. "We wouldn't do it."

With both teams among the nation's best, local promoters knew that a Dunbar–Calvert Hall game at a college arena would be a financial windfall. The previous season's game at the Towson Center on the campus of Towson State University had drawn five thousand spectators. With a national championship at stake this year, some thought that number would double. A number of promoters approached both coaches throughout the season, but no deal had been negotiated.

A week before the Poets traveled to Camden, the Dunbar–Calvert Hall rivalry became a national story when "Two Kings of the Same Hill" by Franz Lidz appeared in *Sports Illustrated*'s February 8 edition.

"When James (Pop) Tubman, the 5'8" point guard for the Calvert Hall College High School Cardinals, isn't moving the ball upcourt with his powerful, rhythmic dribble, he's often flagging down wild passes and shoveling them off behind him to fast-breaking teammates for easy layups. Tyrone (Muggsy) Bogues, a 5'3" playmaker, scoots, skates and skitters for the Dunbar High Poets, picking off passes from hulking opponents like a sparrow stealing seeds from lazy pigeons," Lidz wrote.

"Pop and Muggsy live not far from each other in predominantly black East Baltimore. There, a lot of basketball fans think Dunbar, which at week's end had a 19–0 record, is the best high school team in the country. However, *Basketball Weekly* and just about every other publication that keeps track of such things rank Calvert Hall (21–0) No. 1. *Basketball Weekly* had Dunbar No. 5 in its latest (Jan. 28) poll," the article continued.

"We have nothing to prove," said Amatucci.

Yet, despite Amatucci's assertion, Calvert Hall indeed had

something to prove. Too many people in Baltimore believed that the Cardinals had to beat Dunbar to be the best team in the city, never mind the country.

The Poets had heard all about Billy Thompson, but they'd never seen him play. They were convinced that Reggie Williams was the best player in the country, and they wanted to make sure that after the Camden game, everyone else knew it as well. The Poets knew that, more than likely, they wouldn't be able to get a crack at Calvert Hall, so Camden was going to be their defining proclamation. Despite the fact that they still had the city playoffs approaching at the end of the season, this was going to be their national championship game.

Many people did not share Dunbar's confidence, however. They viewed the Camden contest as an uphill battle for Dunbar, perhaps one they wouldn't be able to overcome, especially considering that the Panthers had not lost a home game since 1977. And it was common knowledge that many nationally ranked schools that traveled to Camden left complaining about one-sided officiating.

Wade was aware of the atmosphere in Camden's gym. In terms of a home-court advantage, it was every bit the equal of Dunbar's own intimidating atmosphere back in Baltimore. He was also aware that some of the officiating in those games had been slanted in Camden's favor, especially when well-regarded teams from out of town traveled to play there.

"I had been on the phone with [Camden coach] Clarence Turner several times and requested that we split up the officiating crew," said Wade. "I just wanted to make sure that we didn't have to play against Camden *and* the referees. I'd heard about some shaky dealings down there with the refs, and I didn't think it was out of line for me to ask for some fairness. I asked him to split the crew up, and out of the three refs that were assigned to work the game, that one of them be from Baltimore. But he refused."

The other factor that the Poets had no control over would be the enthusiastic fan support that Camden enjoyed. They knew that the Poet Followers would be there to support them, and there were rumors that the group had chartered two buses to transport a large group to the game. But they knew that they would be heavily outnumbered.

"Even though we might have only had a few familiar faces in the crowd, just having that support, wherever we went, did wonders for us," said Bogues. "It was an amazing feeling for us to bust out of the locker room for our warm-ups, playing against teams in other states, and see Mr. Ray Short and that Poet Followers group there. It's really hard to explain the level of support they gave us and how cool it was to see them, wearing their Dunbar colors and enthusiastically cheering for us. We knew that our fans would be in the minority, but we also knew that East Baltimore would be in the house."

On Sunday morning, Valentine's Day, February 14, the Poets gathered in the gym to hear a few words from their coach before they went outside to board the bus. Wade was notorious for giving pregame speeches that highlighted how good the other team was. But on the morning of the Camden trip, none of it was contrived. This was going to be the biggest game he'd ever coached in, with national implications, and the Poets knew that this game was going to define their season.

"We were ready to go, and we all felt like this was the biggest game of our lives," said Bogues. "We thrived off challenges and doubts. The anticipation level couldn't get any higher."

As the team walked outside to board Mr. Parran's bus for the final time that season, they were greeted by a throng of well-wishers. They noticed that there were two chartered buses that would bring about sixty Poet Followers to the game. But what they saw behind the buses shocked them.

"There was a caravan of about fifty cars lined up behind the buses, and they would be following us up to Camden," said Goodwin. "There were hundreds of people out there that morning, wearing their maroon and gold. They weren't just out there to wish us luck. They were all coming along for the ride."

CHAPTER ELEVEN

"We're Gonna Have a Party in Here Tonight"

THE TWO-AND-A-HALF-HOUR RIDE FROM East Baltimore, on through Philadelphia, over the Ben Franklin Bridge and across the Delaware River into Camden, was a relatively quiet one. Despite the silence that characterized most of the drive, the boys did not seem nervous. There were snippets of the usual jokes about somebody's haircut or choice of clothes, but an overall intensity pervaded the cabin. The normal sunny and silly disposition that belied the team's toughness was not present on the morning of February 14, 1982. This was a business trip.

"I told the guys to relax while we were en route," said Wade. "I wanted them to get their minds right, close their eyes, and visualize what they wanted to accomplish and how they wanted to execute."

"We were more serious on that ride because nobody had ever talked about another team that we were going to play like the way they talked about Camden," said Reggie Williams. "People talked about them like we were about to play against the Lakers with Magic Johnson and Kareem Abdul-Jabbar. Everybody kept talking about how good they were, how big they were, and how they had the number one player in the entire country. So there wasn't any foolishness on the ride up there. I didn't say one word. I was just playing the game over and over in my mind."

"This was the national stage that we had craved," said Bogues. "And it felt like such a big moment for me because I was going to be matched up against Kevin Walls, who was getting a lot of national publicity. Coach Wade was making him out to be this All-World type of talent. He was left-handed, had some height, and he definitely had a reputation of a guy with some skills at the point guard position. I wasn't just ready to see where I stacked up against him. I was ready to prove that I was better than him. I never wanted for any confidence and felt like there was never a point guard that was better than me."

Camden, like Baltimore, was a relic of what it had been in its days as an industrial and economic powerhouse. Camden was once home to the New York Shipbuilding Corporation, which reached its peak as the world's largest shipyard during World War II. Employing over forty thousand workers, it produced many of the United States Navy's warships and aircraft carriers. The world's largest manufacturer of phonographs and phonograph records, the Victor Talking Machine Company, was headquartered there as well, as was the Campbell Soup Company.

But with the decline of Camden's manufacturing base, the jobs vanished, a pattern similar to that experienced in Baltimore. Racial tensions and riots in the late 1960s and early 1970s deepened the city's decline. As longtime residents with resources fled to other, more attractive South Jersey suburbs, and businesses that could hire and provide stable lives for their workers declined, the illegal drug trade flourished, putting Camden in a decades-long stranglehold. As in many ghetto areas, sports became a rallying point for the community. Camden High School had sent a number of alumni into the National Football League. And Clarence Turner's powerhouse basketball program was a major source of pride in a city that would be designated one of the poorest and most dangerous in America.

As they drove through Camden and up to the school that was known as "the Castle on the Hill" because of its Gothic façade and spires, the Poets were greeted with some visual evidence that this game would be like no other that they'd previously experienced.

"I remember the bus pulling up in front of the school, and as we were getting ready to get off the bus, we saw a limousine drive up," said Bogues. "We started getting excited, wondering who would be riding in a limousine in the ghetto to go to a basketball game. And when the door opened, we saw Billy Thompson get out of it, wearing a tuxedo with a bow tie, with a big smile on his face like he was walking on some red carpet in Hollywood. We were like, 'Man, what in the hell goes on up here?' But that made us angry. We were from the projects, our families were struggling, and this dude was showing up at the game in a limo? We took that as a sign that he was soft. We were talking to one another like, 'Oh, we got something for them today. They must really think they're something special up here.' That really motivated us when we saw that."

As the Poets dressed in the visitors' locker room in the bowels of the building, they heard an incredible commotion taking place above their heads in the upstairs gymnasium. The rowdy tumult alarmed Wade, who dispatched his young son, Darryl, to see what was going on. Darryl scampered up to the gym, where he saw the Camden Panthers putting on a spectacular slam-dunk exhibition in their layup lines. The gym was overflowing with people, and the crowd was already rambunctious about a half-hour before the game started.

Normally, high school players were not allowed to dunk the ball during pregame warm-ups. After Darryl Wade came back downstairs to tell his dad what all the commotion was about, Wade began launching into another rousing, emotional pep talk as the Poets were poised to take the court for their warm-up routine. He began ranting, once again, about Camden's talent, their winning tradition, and their home court winning streak before he was unexpectedly interrupted.

"Mr. Wade, with all due respect, we understand what you're trying to say. But at this point, it's unnecessary. We're ready to play," said the normally quiet Reggie Williams. His teammates' shocked eyes darted back and forth from Reggie to the coach who ruled with an iron fist, wondering how he would react. Williams looked confident, angry, and anxious, like a boxer before the opening bell of a championship bout.

"Mr. Wade, if you don't mind, can we just go upstairs and play the basketball game?" Bogues chimed in, eliciting chuckles from his teammates. "We understand what you're saying. You can finish your talk later."

After scanning the hunger and intensity etched into the faces of his players, Wade inhaled deeply. He smiled and dispatched his team upstairs. But before doing so, he had the final word. "They want to see a show, let's give them a show," he instructed.

Before the Poets made their appearance, the Poet Followers, sporting their maroon-and-gold colors, and other Baltimore fans were booed mercilessly when they entered the gym and began taking whatever seats were available. Although Clarence Turner had arranged for Dunbar to have tickets, there was no specific designated area for them. They could not sit together as a unified cheering section. They would have to disperse themselves throughout the gym and sit among the Camden fans.

"I had been following the Dunbar team all year and was a big fan of Mr. Wade," said Herman Harried, a tenth grader at Eastern High School at the time and a rising young talent on the city's prep basketball scene. He was nicknamed Tree because of his long legs and expansive arms. "To watch Muggsy and Reggie Williams and David Wingate and Reggie Lewis: those guys were just phenomenal to see in person. I was establishing myself as one of the better young players in Baltimore at the time and knew that I was going to transfer into Dunbar the next year. I caught a ride up to Camden with my coach from the Cecil Kirk Recreation Center, Anthony 'Dudie' Lewis, and was part of the big caravan that made the trip, following the team bus. And that place was packed. The Camden fans were arguing with the Dunbar fans, a few fights almost broke out, and Mr. Wade and the guys hadn't even come into the gym to warm up yet. It was a crazy scene. I just found a seat in the crowd and kept my mouth shut before the game started because I wasn't sure what was going to happen. We had a lot of folks from Baltimore who made that trip, but we were significantly outnumbered."

"The energy in that gym was unlike anything we'd ever experienced on the road," said Lynn Badham. "And people were shocked when they saw Muggsy. I remember Sonny Hill, the legendary summer league coach who grew up with Wilt Chamberlain. He was working as a broadcaster with the Philadelphia 76ers at the time and he was there. He was sitting near the scorer's table. He kept talking about Muggsy, calling him 'the little guy' and saying, 'How in the world are they going to beat us with that little guy?' When I heard him talking about 'us,' I felt like saying, 'Who is "us"? You're from Philadelphia, dangblammit, not Camden!' I didn't say anything, though, but that made me upset. There was a lot of electricity and anxiety in that place. Everybody couldn't wait for the game to get started."

When the Poets jogged onto the court, they went about their normal warm-up routine. When they started their layup drills, Muggsy dribbled toward the hoop, jumped high into the air, and rolled in the first layup with his hand dangling at rim level. He was followed by his childhood buddy, the 5-foot-6 backup point guard Darryl "OJ" Wood, who rose from the floor as if propelled by a rocket—and *boom!*—slammed home an improbable, one-handed dunk. *Boom! boom! boom!!* Before half of the Poets got their chance to rattle rims, the crowd swiveled their heads away from the home team's basket, unable to take their eyes off the Dunbar athletes. Even the Panthers, sensing a shift of energy in the gym, turned their heads to see what the Dunbar players were doing.

"Coach told us to go out there and put on a show, so we did exactly that, starting with our layup line," said Bogues. "We were never allowed to dunk during warm-ups, but since Camden was doing it, we put on a pregame show like they had never seen before. We had some high risers on our team who could fly through the air and throw down some mean dunks. OJ was five foot six, but he could dunk easily. Reggie, Tim Dawson, and Gate were awesome dunkers. And our bench guys like Truck and Keith James could sky, too. We gave them something to think about before the game even started with our athleticism, that was for sure."

When the starting lineups were announced, the crowd was already frenzied. The Panthers' starting front line of 6-foot-8 center Jerome White, 6-foot-8 forward Billy Thompson, and 6-foot-6 forward Wesley Fuller was visibly bigger and bulkier than their Poet counterparts. But the size differential truly came into focus when the starting point guards were announced. As Kevin Walls, the 6-foot-2 left-handed sophomore who was being touted among the country's best, was introduced to the crowd, the roar was almost deafening. When Reggie Williams, David Wingate, Gary Graham, and Tim Dawson were introduced for the Poets, the Panther fans seemed uninterested while the Baltimore contingent clapped and hollered. But when the muffled words "And starting at point guard for Dunbar, 5-foot-3-inch junior Tyrone Bogues" came floating out of the gym's speakers, Muggsy jogged onto the court to a cacophony of taunts and laughter.

"Not only was it the people I was sitting near in the bleachers, but practically every Camden fan in the gym starting laughing at Muggsy," said Harried. "I couldn't believe that. I was really amused, too, because I thought they would have known about Muggsy. But they obviously didn't. They were clapping and dancing like they'd just heard the funniest joke ever. It shocked me. They kept saying stuff like, 'Who is that little boy?' and 'Kevin Walls is going to destroy him!' They just laughed and were having a good old time during the player introductions. I didn't say a word and just smiled. I knew that they had no idea what they were in for. Those Camden folks had never seen him before, and I guess they figured that they were going to have an easy victory handed to them."

Most people who had seen him play in Baltimore stopped noticing how short he was after only a few minutes of action. But every time the Poets traveled outside of the city, crowds were invariably stunned at the sight of Dunbar's diminutive floor general. The thing that enraged Bogues at Camden was that it wasn't merely the fans. The opposing players and coaches were all joking and laughing as well.

"Well, I didn't find that to be one bit funny," said Bogues. "Coach Wade always told us to respect our opponents. And during the introductions and right before the game started, those guys were disrespecting me."

"Obviously, their coaches didn't scout us, because if they had, they would have known that Muggsy was a remarkable player, no matter how small he was, and they would not have been laughing," said Reggie Williams. "He might have been the shortest guy on the floor, but he had more skill and heart than all of those Camden guys put together. And Walls laughing at Muggs, walking around bragging that he was going to Louisville to play his college ball, even though he was only a sophomore, was inexcusable. But I kind of got a kick out of it, because I knew what happened to people who made Muggsy angry. And I knew that those Camden guys weren't going to be doing any laughing or bragging once the game started."

Kevin Walls walked over, pointed to his diminutive opponent, and chuckled along with the fans in the stands. He even went so far as to pantomime a patronizing pat on Muggsy's head, as if he were a pet. The crowd once again erupted in laughter. Jogging back to the sidelines for the team huddle with his head momentarily bowed, moments before tip-off, Bogues was met by Wade.

"Are you okay, little man?" the coach gently asked his point guard.

Bogues lifted his eyes from the floor exposing a Cheshire cat's grin.

"Mr. Wade, I am just fine," he told his coach. "And when the game is over, I'm gonna have the last laugh. We're gonna have a party in here tonight."

"That was the type of situation I loved," said Bogues. "Anyone who underestimated me was in trouble."

The Poets noticed that in addition to their own fans, there was another contingent from Baltimore who made the trip, a small group that was undoubtedly rooting for them to lose. Calvert Hall Head Coach Mark Amatucci and his assistant coaches were also in attendance. Their presence added even more fuel to the internal fire raging inside the Dunbar players.

"In addition to simply wanting to win the game, we all wanted to send a message to Amatucci and the Calvert Hall coaches as well," said Wade.

"I said it before and I'm gonna say it again," Wade instructed his players as they huddled together, before sending them onto the court to start the game. "They came here to see a show, and that is just what we're going to give them. We're going to give them some Poetry in Motion. When this game is over, they are going to know what we mean when we say, 'Poet Pride!' Everybody get your hands in."

The boys stacked their hands on top of Wade's and chanted: "One, two, three, *Defense!!!*"

Camden won the opening tip. As Walls began dribbling up the court, Muggsy stole the ball from him and zipped a bullet of a pass to a streaking Reggie Williams, who slammed it home. The resounding echo of the dunk reverberated through the stunned silence of Camden's crowd, accentuated by a smattering of muffled statements of "Oh, shit!"

Before Walls could dribble the ball over to half-court on the ensuing possession, Bogues swiped the ball from him again and swiftly sped downcourt, floating a divine alley-oop lob pass that was jammed violently through the rim by a soaring David Wingate. The patronizing smile on the face of the highly recruited

Walls, so gleefully on display during the player introductions, was quickly replaced by a stricken look of panic. Clarence Turner made an adjustment, instructing his other players to bring the ball upcourt as he realized that Muggsy's tenacious defensive ability was something that he hadn't planned for. Without Walls as Camden's primary ball handler, the Panthers were already in a situation that they were not accustomed to.

Bogues commented, "After those first two steals and slam dunks, nobody in that gym, including [Walls], was laughing at me anymore. He didn't understand who I was before the game started. But he definitely understood who I was and what my game was all about when he started touching the basketball at the beginning of the game."

With three minutes elapsed in the first quarter, Camden led by a score of 7 to 6. But spurred by their defensive pressure, Dunbar ripped off one of their patented spurts, a 14–2 dash that gave them a 20–9 lead with 1:28 left to play in the opening stanza. On defense, they executed their game plan to perfection, nullifying Camden's fast break and confusing them with the speed and effective traps that characterized their aggressive 2–1–2 zone. The Panthers would turn the ball over twelve times in the first half alone. At the end of the quarter, Dunbar's lead was 27–13.

"That game was over midway through the first quarter," said Badham. "It was an utter annihilation! Muggsy was stealing the ball left and right, they couldn't get anything going against our defense, and our offense was unstoppable. Muggsy was just phenomenal. I was supposed to be keeping stats, but I was in awe of the performance we put on. We played the game of basketball on that day, against one of the best teams in the country, better than any high school team that I had ever seen. To come in that hostile place and play as well as they did, it was a testament to Muggsy's brilliance. On defense, he changed the game. And when we were on offense, he made the right decision on every play, making sure the ball got into the hands of the right player at the right time. We were operating on all cylinders. From the moment the game started and on through the end of the first quarter, those Camden people knew what we had known all along. No matter how good a team might be, nobody was better than that Dunbar team. Nobody!"

Dunbar held Camden to 8 points in the second quarter and went to the locker room at halftime with a 50–21 lead. They continually beat Camden at its own game, scoring easy baskets in transition. When they weren't racing down the court to corral Muggsy's passes for easy slam dunks, they were sinking deep shots from the perimeter and converting from the midrange as well. Overall, the Poets shot 62 percent from the field during the first two quarters. Unable to score in transition or solve Dunbar's half-court defensive pressure, Camden converted a mere 9 of their 24 shot attempts in the first half.

In the second half, the Panthers began yelling and fighting with one another as Bogues ran circles around them. Wingate put on a dazzling shooting performance, converting 14 of his 18 shot attempts en route to his game-high total of 31 points. In the first half, he rendered Camden's 2–3 zone useless by making eight straight long-distance jump shots. Reggie Williams spent most of the first half on the bench with foul trouble, but Reggie Lewis filled in with some inspired play. Williams exploded for 19 points in the second half to finish with 22, while also grabbing a team-high 9 rebounds.

Billy Thompson, who came into the game averaging over 32 points per game, scored 24, but he was never a factor. On four separate occasions, when an entry pass into Thompson on the low block proved successful and the big man attempted to initiate a move toward the basket, Muggsy swooped down to the baseline to strip the ball from him. By the fourth quarter, the Dunbar starters were resting comfortably on the bench, gleefully cheering on the substitutes. When the carnage ended, Dunbar had won 84–59. Bogues tallied 15 points, 12 assists, and 6 steals. Gary Graham added 8 points, while Reggie Lewis and Eric Green scored 6 and 2 points respectively. For Camden, Kevin Walls scored an inconsequential 8 points. The Panthers' big center, Jerome White, scored 6 while their other star forward, Wesley Fuller, scored 9.

"For years, the gymnasium at Camden High School has been one of the most feared places in the country for visiting teams, a veritable chamber of horrors where opponents encountered tough Camden teams, intimidating fans and alleged home-cooked officiating," wrote Bernie Miklasz in the next day's edition of the *News-American*. "Since 1977, Camden had lost just one game in the gym that sits on a dark, unattractive campus in the middle of a high-crime district. Visiting teams come here expecting the worst and usually get it. On Saturday afternoon, unbeaten Dunbar paid a visit to the chamber of horrors. And in one of the most awesome performances ever given by a Baltimore high school basketball team, the second-ranked Poets put on a clinic. Storming to a 50–21 lead at the half, Dunbar went on to rout the Panthers 84–59, shattering both the mystique of the Camden basketball team and the gymnasium in which it plays."

Sonny Hill might have doubted Bogues before the game, but he was quoted afterward as saying, "That was the Philadelphia 76ers out there wearing Dunbar's maroon-and-gold uniforms today."

When it became apparent to the Camden crowd that Dunbar

was not going to be beaten, they accepted the fact that they were in for a humiliating defeat. Amazingly, they began to appreciate the brilliant performance they were watching. On several occasions, they gave Muggsy a standing ovation. The Camden crowd stood on their feet, chanting loudly, "MUGGSY! MUGGSY!" before rushing the court at the final buzzer. The same people who had laughed at the young man wound up storming the court at the game's conclusion, deluging him for autographs.

"It was pretty amazing to watch the crowd's conversion," said Harried. "To see them going from teasing and laughing at him, to them giving him a standing ovation and cheering for him, it's something that I'll never forget. The people I was sitting with started asking me questions about him; they wanted to know all about him. They fell in love with him and began showing him the respect that he deserved."

"Dunbar is the best basketball team I have ever seen," Camden Head Coach Clarence Turner said after the game.

"The way we performed and demolished them, that was a special moment because they really were a great team," said Williams. "I wanted to show everybody that I wasn't just one of the best players in Baltimore, but one of the best in the country. And I did that. And Muggsy proved the same thing. We were on a mission to prove a point and show the world who we were. Everybody did their job to perfection. Coach Wade had us incredibly prepared, and we sent a message out to the entire country. It was one of the most special and rewarding nights of my entire life."

Having now played Dunbar and Calvert Hall, the top-ranked team in Baltimore and in the entire country that season, Turner had no doubts about who the best team in the nation was. "Dunbar is twenty points better than Calvert Hall," he told the *News-American*'s Miklasz. "And if the game is properly officiated,

Dunbar might beat them by twenty-five or thirty points. That little point guard of theirs is better than [Calvert Hall point guard] Pop Tubman. Their big people are much better than [Calvert Hall center] Duane Ferrell or anybody that Calvert Hall has up front. No team has ever beaten us like that in this gym or any damn place."

On the bus ride back home, the team celebrated, did their chants, and recounted the steals, passes, slam dunks, and jump shots they made during their dominating performance. They high-fived and complimented one another on their accomplishment, but the atmosphere was not as ebullient as one would expect. As Wade sat in the front of the bus, he beamed with pride, turning his head to laugh at the stories and jokes being told.

"We had a great time coming back, but we didn't celebrate as if we'd won a world championship," said Wade. "I think everyone had invested so much of themselves, it was so emotional that the party was somewhat subdued after we won. After about thirty minutes or so, things just got quiet, some guys started napping. I congratulated them and told them to savor it, because it was a feat that people who saw it would never forget. There was a magnitude to what we had done. But I also reminded them that we could enjoy it, but we needed to turn the page the minute we got back in the gym. We had a game coming up on Tuesday, and then it was on to the city public school tournament to wrap up the season. They understood the goal, which was to win our remaining games. But beating Camden the way we did, it was the biggest win of the year for all of us. East Baltimore, and the city as a whole, would celebrate the win much longer than we did."

In the Monday edition of the *News-American*, Miklasz wrote a column that upset many people whose loyalties were with Calvert Hall. Entitled "Who's #1, Calvert Hall or Dunbar? Poets Have Proven They Belong," it asked a compelling question about the national basketball rankings. He argued that writers from national magazines like *Street & Smith's* and *Basketball Weekly*, who had seen Calvert Hall play in two tournaments and had never seen Dunbar play, were in no position to rank them in the way that the Baltimore writers were, as those local writers had spent an entire season covering and watching both teams play.

Addressing the argument that Calvert Hall played more of a national schedule, Miklasz countered that Dunbar had neither the resources nor permission from the city's public school governing athletic body to compete in games all over the country. He then pointed out their one common opponent, Camden, and contrasted Calvert Hall's 5-point, come-from-behind victory at a neutral site with Dunbar's 25-point blowout on the Panthers' home court.

He pointed out that Lake Clifton, despite being crushed twice by the Poets, losing by more than 30 points both times, hadn't lost another game locally all year, and that the Lakers' other defeat, a double-overtime nail-biter, came at the hands of Washington, DC's Dunbar High School, which was the fifth-ranked team on the East Coast at the time by *Eastern Basketball* magazine. After the Poets humiliated the talented Camden team, Miklasz argued that the Poets could no longer be considered the second-best team in the city.

"To some, it may be wrong to make Calvert Hall—a team that has done everything asked of it this season—relinquish its sole possession of the top spot," he concluded. "But to keep Dunbar in the second spot is a far greater injustice."

"I knew, after our performance against Camden, that Amatucci would not put his undefeated record on the line against us," said Wade. "He had to say the right things and make it seem like they wanted to play us and settle the thing once and for all. But deep down, we all knew that he wasn't going to give us a shot. He had too much to lose."

Resigned to the thought that the Calvert Hall game would not happen, despite the continued posturing in the media, Wade focused in on the things he could control, getting his team ready to close out their season.

CHAPTER TWELVE

"True Power of That Orange Ball"

BACK IN BALTIMORE, THE Poets didn't have much time to bask in the glory of their epic victory over Camden. There was only one day of practice before their final regular season game against Northern High School that Tuesday. The Baltimore City Public Schools Tournament was set to begin on Thursday.

"I had to make sure that the guys weren't feeling too high about what they'd done, because we still had some goals that we wanted to accomplish," said Wade. "We had some unfinished business on the local level. So it was back to work as usual, as if the Camden game never happened, as far as I was concerned. I definitely downplayed their success and found fault in as much as I could to keep them focused."

The Poets' practice might have been business as usual, but the mood in the hallways and classrooms, as well as on the neighborhood streets and in the city's larger basketball community was much more celebratory.

"The outcome of that game really did lift the spirits of many people throughout the city," said Marshall Goodwin. "No one really believed that they could go up to New Jersey and dominate the way they did because, you have to understand, Camden had such a huge reputation and mystique at the time. All of the hype was about this great Camden team and the guy who all of the so-called basketball experts said was the best player in the country. So the word spread like wildfire, and the anticipation was really building up. People kept saying, 'Damn, they beat Billy Thompson and them! What are they gonna do next?' "

Wade dialed up the pressure during Monday's practice, but there were no signs of complacency among the players. During the school day, they regaled their classmates with stories about the game against Camden. They talked about how Muggsy was booed and laughed at, only to be given a standing ovation and swarmed at the game's end. They reenacted, in slow motion, the vicious slam dunks that Wingate, Williams, and Dawson performed. They basked in the adulation, high fives, and pats on the back that their peers and teachers greeted them with. People stopped them on the street to shake their hands, to thank them. But once Wade blew his whistle, the boys seemed to attack the bricks and sandbags and running and drills with an even greater fervor, wearing their bruises, bloodied elbows, and floor burns with greater pride.

"We didn't come into that next practice on a high from the Camden game," said Reggie Williams. "We celebrated on the bus ride back, but that was about it. We went at it hard in that practice, the same way that we always did. Whenever we stepped on the court, we expected excellence and played as if it would be the last time we ever played. Mr. Wade was intense, but at the same time, we knew that we wanted to accomplish our goals. And those were to win the city championship and the 'A' Conference championship and finish the season undefeated."

The Poets knew that they would eventually play Lake Clifton again. Even though they had thrashed them twice earlier in the season, they knew that the Lakers were still a solid team that had defeated them in the public school championship game the year prior. And their hunger to avenge that game had yet to be satisfied.

For Muggsy, the basketball court was even more of a sanctuary than usual as Dunbar approached the season's closing stretch. At the time, there was a situation in his family that pulled his concentration away from its normal orbit of girls, jokes, schoolwork, and hoops. He'd temporarily moved out of his family's apartment in the Lafayette Projects to live with his aunt in the nearby public housing development that was known in the neighborhood as "the New Projects" on Monument Street. There had been a few incidents with his aunt's boyfriend becoming physically aggressive and abusive toward her. And that situation had escalated. So Bogues started going over with more frequency to check on her.

"The guy was on drugs, and his behavior was becoming more and more erratic," said Bogues. "Eventually, I brought some of my clothes and stuff over there and started spending more time there. When I was around, the guy was cool for the most part. But there was one incident when I was there. He started getting loud, being disrespectful, puffing out his chest like he was about to hit my aunt. I stepped in the middle of all that. He tried to test me, and I had to put it on him. I had him choked up in a matter of seconds with an old wrestling move, and that ended that. That was the one and only time I had to get physical with the guy."

There was also an incident one night that sent a momentary panic through city basketball fans and Reggie Williams's family.

As Leon Howard sat in the Lafayette Recreation Center, two young boys came sprinting through the doors looking panic-stricken.

"Fat Man, Russ got shot. Somebody shot Reggie; we just heard it on the radio," one of them said, out of breath.

"What? What do you mean Reggie got shot?" Howard asked.

"We were just listening to the radio, and they said a black teenager named Reggie Williams got shot dead near Johns Hopkins Hospital," the other boy replied.

Howard looked at his watch. It was after 8:00 p.m.

"Shit, they shot somebody else named Reggie Williams then, because if they didn't shoot him at home, then it wasn't Russ," said Howard. "Russ don't leave the damn house. He's home right now. I guarantee it."

Howard knew that Williams was a notorious homebody who, if he wasn't at practice or at the rec center, was resting comfortably at home, watching TV, hanging out with his family, and eating. He hustled into his office and hurriedly picked up the phone. But when Williams's mother answered, she said that Reggie hadn't returned home yet. Panicked, Howard told her what he'd heard. They both began frantically calling all over the neighborhood, asking if anybody had seen Reggie over the past few hours.

"I got home not too long after Mr. Howard had called my mother," said Williams. "And my house was in an uproar. My mother started yelling at me, asking, 'Where the hell you been?' She was scared that something had happened to me. When I told her that I stopped over to the house of the girl that I was dating, she calmed down. But for a little while there, the word was spreading through the neighborhood grapevine that I'd gotten shot."

Within a few minutes, Howard's phone at the rec center rang.

"Hey, Fat Man, it's Russ," Williams said, sounding relaxed on the other line. "I just got home and my mom told me you called. You got everybody going crazy over here, talking about somebody shot me. You know I don't run the streets, man. Ain't nothing happen to me."

"Gotdammit, some boy named Reggie Williams got killed out here in East Baltimore tonight," Howard said, relieved. "It was on the radio. I figured it couldn't be you, because you don't never leave the damn house. But when I called over there and your mom said you wasn't home, I got worried."

"I'm okay, Fat Man," Williams told him. "I'll stop over to the rec and see you soon."

Howard's wife also told him that he'd received another phone call around that time, one that he wasn't so interested in returning with any expediency.

"She told me Bob Wade had called, that he wanted me to call him back, and that he sounded serious," said Howard. "I was like, 'Aw, what the hell does he want?' It was no secret that our relationship at the time was a little strained. He didn't trust me because I was close to all the college coaches, and he knew that. And Muggsy and Reggie would come over to the rec center all the time to hang out and talk to me. Those college coaches would come over to my house whenever they were in Baltimore. Of course, they'd try to butter me up and ask me if I could help a kid go to their school. In the recruiting game, everybody was trying to get an edge, no matter how small. So Bob would call me from time to time and say, 'I heard so-and-so came to see you,' talking about one of the coaches. It seemed like he had eyes everywhere. He'd try to intimidate me, and I'd say, 'What the hell do you want?' He'd tell me he wanted to make sure that nothing tricky was going on with the recruitment that would get the kids jammed up."

But Howard knew exactly what Wade was calling about this time. Lefty Driesell, Maryland's head basketball coach, had recently sent a shipment of Terrapins practice jerseys to the Lafayette Recreation Center.

"Lefty didn't send twenty jerseys like some of the other schools did," said Howard. "He sent us hundreds! I couldn't keep all of them, because they would have just sat there in a box. So I gave them away to all of the kids in the projects who would come into the rec center."

When Wade noticed the proliferation of Maryland jerseys, his antennae rose. When he asked a bunch of boys whom he'd seen on the street where they'd gotten them from, they informed him that Mr. Howard was giving them away at the Lafayette Recreation Center.

"Lefty was a helluva recruiter," said Wade. "And he wanted Wingate and Reggie Williams really bad. When I saw all those kids in East Baltimore wearing those red Maryland jerseys, I was pissed off. I knew something was up. So I called Leon and told him that he'd better not be doing anything for Lefty. Because the last thing I wanted was the NCAA sniffing around and causing problems for my kids."

"The NCAA had actually called me a couple of times," said Howard. "But there wasn't any foul play. I'd answer their questions and that was it. But Bob was pissed. He cursed me out and called me every name in the book. I told him that I took the shirts, but I never told Reggie that he should be thinking about going to Maryland, and I never had any secret deal to influence him to go to Maryland. When Lefty said he was going to send me some jerseys for my guys at the rec center, I was cool with that. Coaches from a bunch of different programs would send us old practice jerseys and even game uniforms."

But Wade was more concerned about a possible emotional letdown in Dunbar's regular season finale. Those concerns were assuaged in Monday's practice, though.

When the team bus pulled into the Northern High School parking lot on Tuesday, Wade was surprised at the crowd that he saw outside of the entrance to the school's gym.

"I guess the word had gotten out about Camden, so with the crowd that showed up, not only at Northern, but for all of our remaining games, there was even more electricity in the air," said Wade. "The gyms were always packed when we played, but it was like things shot up to an entirely different level. I saw faces in those crowds that I'd never seen before. There were a lot more white faces, too. People were coming in, not only from the surrounding counties, but from all over the state to get a look at us. And they were coming in droves. Folks from DC and Virginia and Philadelphia were showing up hours early so they could get into the games. I'd never seen anything like it."

In their last warm-up before the city tournament, as six more inches of snow fell in Baltimore, the Poets were confident that they'd win their twenty-fourth game in a row. But Northern played an inspired first half and proved that they were up for the challenge, at least during the game's first sixteen minutes.

But the Poets ambushed Northern with a suffocating defensive effort in the second half, limiting them to just 8 points in the third quarter, followed by a mere 7 in the fourth. The final score was 76–46, with Reggie Williams's stellar 26-point, 10-rebound performance augmented by Wingate's 18 points and 11 rebounds.

During the next day's practice, as the players expected, Wade was on the warpath. Drill after drill was laced with his shouts and profanities. He tore into the reserve units and chastised the starters, railing against complacency.

"We play the game the right way," Wade screamed. "That means finding that extra gear that the other team doesn't have. That means sacrificing, mastering the fundamentals, doing the small things. If you have a teammate ahead of you who is open, even if he's only a few steps ahead, you pass him the ball. Everybody is talking about you on the evening news programs. There are articles in the newspaper every day with your pictures. The politicians are all showing up at our games, smiling, giving you hugs and shaking your hands, treating you like you're some damn movie stars. I'm starting to think you guys believe all that bullshit. You were terrible in the first half yesterday. Atrocious! That was a far cry from what we strive for every day in practice. What is it? Do we have to play teams that people think are better than us in order to play our best ball? Gary, David, and the rest of you seniors—there are no more tomorrows. This is it for you guys. What is your legacy going to be? The same way they talk about the teams from the 1950s around here, the same way they still talk about Skip Wise and Larry Gibson and Ernie Graham, no matter what happens after you guys go off to college, people in this city will still be talking about you forty years from now. So do you want to be known as one of the best teams this city has ever seen? Or do you want to be known as one of those good teams that just sat on the toilet and couldn't shit?"

The next evening, Thursday, February 18, hundreds of people were stranded outside on the icy streets, unable to gain entrance to the Dunbar gym. It was the Poets' final home game of the season, their opening round playoff game in the city public schools tournament against Douglass High School. Prior to the team taking the court for their warm-ups, Wade paced back and forth in the home locker room.

"This is the last game that we'll play in our own gym this year," he said calmly, a seemingly different person altogether from the raving maniac who ran the previous practice. "You seniors, go out there and cherish this moment. You guys won't realize how much fun and how rewarding these experiences are until years from now, when it hits you how special it was and what an honor it was to play in this gym, to wear this uniform, and to be supported by all of those people who are waiting upstairs to see you play."

Wade then walked to the chalkboard and wrote down the number 49.

"They better not score more than forty-nine points," he said, smiling. "We have three games in four days before we win this tournament. So I want the starters to wear these guys out early so the reserves can take care of their business in the second half. I want everybody well rested so we can be playing at our maximum abilities over these next few days. Now let's go out there and have fun. Play our game. Give our fans a show at our final home game. And let's finish the job that we started when we got together on that first day of practice, when Muggsy was crying like a little baby 'cause those bricks were kicking his ass!"

The locker room erupted in laughter.

Reggie Williams led them again with a strong 26-point, 11-rebound performance. Wingate was equally impressive, chipping in with 24 points as the Poets romped past Douglass 98–51 and advanced to the next day's semifinal game against Carver Vocational Technical High School, which would be played at Morgan State University's Hill Field House.

In the postgame locker room, as the boys shifted their attention to the next game, Wade called for everyone's attention. He pointed to the number 49 that he'd written on the chalkboard prior to the game.

"We didn't reach our goal, fellas," he said.

———

Resting at home one day as the season wound down, Reggie Williams was passing the time doing what he loved best, just lounging around and watching television. In the basketball community, he might have been considered a huge star with a chance to one day make millions in the NBA. But at home, he was far from that.

"My younger brothers, Ivan and Melvin, they weren't into basketball at all," said Williams. "My sister, Veronica, she didn't come to any of my games. My mom never came to any of my games, either. My father would come from time to time, but we never talked about it. I never looked into the stands when I was playing. But sometimes, I'd walk over to the bench for a time-out, and I'd see my dad sitting one row behind Coach Wade. He'd never tell me he was coming, and he didn't come all the time. But I'd see him at some of my games. And he never, ever said anything to me like, 'You had a good game.' So, inside my house, I had the same status as everybody else. My exploits on the basketball court meant nothing."

As he sat in his room watching *Soul Train*, his mother knocked on his door. He noticed a pained look on her face and asked her what was wrong.

"All of a sudden, she just broke down and started crying," said Williams. "I was very close with my mother, but she'd never shared how much she struggled to keep everything together. But that day, she was sobbing. She was telling me about how she just didn't have any money and didn't know how we were going to make it. It was like she had been so brave and so strong for so long, I'd never seen her being vulnerable like that."

Williams stood up and hugged his mother as tightly as he could, her muffled cries absorbed by his chest.

"I just told her that everything was going to be okay," said

Williams. "We just hugged for a long time and I told her, 'Mom, we've made it this far. I just need you to give me a few more years, and I promise that I'm going to take care of everything. As soon as I finish college, you won't have to worry ever again about not having enough money to do what needs to be done. Just give me a couple of years, and I'm going to take it from there. Everything is going to work out. Trust me.' She stopped crying, looked up at me and smiled, and said, 'Okay.' From that moment on, I was even more driven. I'd always dreamed about playing pro ball, ever since I'd watched Earl Monroe with the Bullets and Dr. J with the 76ers. But my desire became even stronger. I didn't know if I was going to make it to the NBA, but I knew that somehow, some way, I needed to do the best I could because I made that promise to take care of my mother."

––––

At Hill Field House on Saturday night, where the seating capacity was 4,250, the boisterous crowd was standing room only for the city playoffs' semifinal matchup. The Poets went for the jugular immediately against Carver, with their pressure defense causing 7 first-quarter turnovers.

"We wanted to knock them out early," said Williams. "We wanted to be on the bench early in the second half so our home-boys could get out there in front of that crowd and get their work in as well."

David Wingate connected on 9 of his 15 shots en route to scoring 25 points to lead the team, and Gary Graham, Tim Dawson, and Reggie Williams combined to score 36 as Dunbar advanced to the tournament final with their 78–53 victory. But Wade was again exasperated with the defensive effort of his reserve units, which allowed Carver to score 36 points in the second half.

"If we'd had a practice or two before the city championship game, we probably would have been doing a whole lot of running with those bricks," said Eric Green. "But luckily, we were playing again the next night. Coach Wade was not happy with the fact that after holding them to single digits in the first and second quarters, the effort of the guys off the bench in the second half didn't match up. And we had our biggest rival, Lake Clifton, coming up, and we knew that we had to be more focused and intense."

Despite their two 30-point victories against them earlier in the year, the Poets remained wary of the Lake Clifton team. The East Baltimore rivalry between the two schools always evoked passion on both sides. And the Lakers were still in the midst of their own impressive season, despite the previous blowouts they'd suffered to Dunbar.

"We got our butts beat soundly by them both times, and we'd like to prove that we're better than those sixty-four points," Lake Clifton's coach, Woody Williams, said about Dunbar, after his team squeaked by Walbrook High School 54–53 to advance to the championship game.

Wade expected a spirited effort from Lake Clifton this time around and made sure that his players understood the magnitude of the task at hand.

"What happened before is history," Wade said in the locker room after their semifinal victory over Carver as he turned the Poets' attention to the game plan for the championship game. "They'll be psyched up and ready to prove that they can play with us. Woody is a great coach, and he'll have some different wrinkles from when we played them at the Poet-Laker Invitational and during the regular season. But you guys have worked incredibly hard and are prepared for any and everything that they're gonna throw at us. Rest up tonight. There's nothing to talk about in terms of strategy at this point. We're going to play Poet basketball tomorrow night, that's all I can say. Do not, I repeat, do not even think about what we did to them before. That means nothing now. You know what the Dunbar–Lake Clifton rivalry is all about. Throw the records out of the window. They're gonna come out swinging tomorrow and give it everything they've got. They're gonna compete. But we're gonna knock their ass out. Now let's get on the bus and go home."

That next day, on Sunday afternoon, fans showed up hours ahead of the game's scheduled 6:30 p.m. tip-off.

"Most people didn't bother to change out of their church clothes on Sunday before they came to that championship game at Morgan," said Goodwin. "People had on their best suits and dresses, and they were all packed in there together like a can of sardines. And the way they were dressed, it was almost like they were showing their respect, like they wanted to show up at the title game looking their fanciest. It was the talk of the city, with all of the politicians and big shots in attendance, too."

Early in the championship game, it was apparent that the Lake Clifton team was inspired. At halftime, they trailed by only 7 points. And in spite of Wade's motivational screaming during the intermission, the Lakers got off to a strong start in the third quarter. For the first time all season, Dunbar found itself in a close game against a local opponent heading into the fourth quarter.

The Poets played uncharacteristically tight in the third period, committing 5 turnovers and missing 10 of their 15 shot attempts. With one minute remaining in the period, the score was tied at 43. As the teams huddled before the start of the fourth quarter, Wade's intensity was palpable, but he spoke calmly, even breaking out a smile on the sidelines.

"We knew that they were gonna give us a game," he told his

players. "And they did. But this is why, this situation right here, is why we ran all those miles with those bricks and those sandbags. Nobody is in better condition than us. Nobody can deal with the pressure we apply down the stretch. They've had their fun. But now, it's our turn. This is where we knock them out. Let's kick some ass and have some fun of our own. This is our time. Poet Pride! Let's go!"

"We'd played a great game up until that point," said Lake Clifton's Carl Fair. "We thought we had them on their heels when we broke our huddle to start the fourth quarter. We could taste it. We felt like we were about to get our revenge for how bad they beat us in those earlier games. But Muggsy obviously didn't care about how we felt or what we thought we were going to do. He just took the game over and put on his own little show."

The fourth quarter belonged entirely to the Poets, due to the brilliance of the smallest player on the court. With six minutes left in the game, leading 47–45, Bogues went to work. Dunbar ran away with the victory, thanks to a closing 16–2 spurt, orchestrated entirely by their point guard. It was a masterful performance. He grabbed 2 steals and caused 3 more Lake Clifton turnovers with his frenetic on-ball defense.

"I remember Muggs kept hollering at me, 'Turn him, G! Turn him!'" said Gary Graham. "He would yell that to me and David when we were guarding guys on the perimeter. Muggs would be studying guys the entire game, timing their dribbles, watching how they pivoted with the ball, stuff like that. He was a genius. So when he said, 'Turn him,' he was telling us to make the guy change his direction. And as soon as the guy would pivot or try to change direction, Muggsy would time it perfectly, be right there to steal his dribble, and we'd be off and running. And as soon as Muggs got his hands on the ball, Coach Wade would be screaming at us, 'Push it, Honey! Fill it, Honey!' telling us to fill the lanes."

The Poets were leading 53–45 with a little more than four minutes remaining, and Bogues worked two minutes off the clock with a dribbling display that was reminiscent of a Harlem Globetrotters routine. The Lake Clifton defenders flailed unsuccessfully, trying to foul him, but Bogues dribbled straight through and around the defensive pressure before delivering astonishing passes that bewildered the opposing players and fans.

"My goodness, Muggsy was unstoppable," said Wade. "He was fantastic. We were running what we called our 'Stack' offense to close out the game. Basically, the other guys were stacked at the elbows and Muggsy was free to dribble and dart around. We have various permutations and patterns to it, different spots that the other guys would get to once Muggsy initiated some of his moves. But it was almost like he was out there by himself. They couldn't lay a hand on him. I've never seen anyone who could dribble the ball like that and put on a show the way he did at the end of that game."

"Muggsy had everybody in the stands going crazy," said Reggie Williams. "The applause was thunderous. Just when it looked like Lake Clifton had him surrounded, he'd squirt out or throw a crazy pass that led to a wide-open dunk. My man was showing off! And the crowd loved it. They gave him three or four standing ovations. It was an amazing performance."

On one play, when two Laker guards seemingly had him blanketed with nowhere to turn, he split the trap with a funky body wiggle and stunning ball control, as if the basketball were a yo-yo on a string. As he sped toward the basket and away from the shocked defenders who appeared to have had him surrounded, Bogues went between his legs with a blur of a quick dribble and delivered a precise, swift, and sudden no-look pass that caught Wingate in perfect stride. As Wingate flew through the air to drop the ball in the basket, the crowd jumped out of their seats in disbelief.

"We called a time-out and I gave my players specific instructions to foul Bogues," Lakers' coach Woody Williams said after the game. "But they couldn't catch him. They couldn't get near him."

Reggie Williams, one of the many Poets who were beneficiaries of Bogues's telepathic passing, led the Poets with 23 points and 9 rebounds. Williams's defense, along with contributions from Wingate, Dawson, and Reggie Lewis, hounded Lakers' star Melvin Mathis into a woeful 4-for-13 shooting performance. Mathis finished with 14 points, well below his season average.

Gary Graham and Wingate both scored 16 points as well. Despite scoring only 2 points, which raised his three-game tournament total to a mere 10 points, Bogues was chosen as the tournament MVP.

"The beauty in Muggsy's game was that he didn't have to score in order for us to be successful," said Reggie Williams. "He cared about winning and could care less about how many points he scored. His defense, his passing, the way he orchestrated our fast break, his entire game and skill set were truly unbelievable. And he was a born leader. I'd played with him my whole life, and it's hard to measure the chemistry we had and how we were able to make each other better. He never ceased to amaze me."

"The talent, top to bottom on our team was unreal," said Graham. "But the thing that truly separated us from everybody else was Muggsy. The year before, we might have panicked in a close situation with the clock running down. That was exactly what happened when we lost that triple-overtime game to Calvert Hall the year before. But with the little fella running our offense and handling the ball, we were never worried about the other team. Muggs was the ultimate weapon. We were all relaxed because we knew—and everybody else who played against us knew—that Shorty was the man."

With the Baltimore City Public Schools Tournament settled, there was one more game on the schedule. The Poets were slated to play in the MSA "A" Conference championship game the next Saturday at the Baltimore Civic Center.

The Civic Center held a special allure for the boys. They knew it was the former home of the Baltimore Bullets, who had relocated to Washington, DC. They also knew it was where Skip Wise put on his most spectacular show when he starred for Dunbar and the Poets beat Adrian Dantley and DeMatha. Now they wanted to etch their names in the city's hoops history in the famed arena.

"We all knew that the Civic Center was Earl 'the Pearl' Monroe's home before he was traded away to the Knicks," said Reggie Williams. "I remember, before I got into basketball, how my uncles would get excited to go down there and watch the Bullets' games. We all looked forward to stepping on that court. To us, it didn't get any bigger than playing in the Civic Center."

The opponent in that final game would once again be Lake Clifton, a matchup of the conference's two top teams.

"Even though it was the last game on our schedule, we honestly felt like our season wasn't going to end after the final game against Lake Clifton," said Bogues. "In our minds, this was going to be the next-to-last hurdle before we finally got our hands on Calvert Hall."

Wade, however, knew better.

"It was apparent to me that, despite all of his posturing in the paper, Amatucci wasn't going to put his undefeated season on the line against us," said Wade. "He kept saying that he'd play us after Calvert Hall played in the Alhambra Tournament, but he knew that meant that we'd have to wait a month. And at that point, we'd be in the spring athletic season. I told him in negotiations, in no uncertain terms, that we wouldn't wait for a month. He'd been at that Camden game to scout us. He knew the deal. If I were in his shoes, I wouldn't have wanted to play us, either."

Wade knew that the upcoming game would be the final one of the season.

———

When the Poets took the floor inside the Civic Center on Saturday, February 27, among the thousands in attendance, there was one fan in particular who inspired them. David Wingate's paralyzed mother, Mattie, was in the audience. It was the first time that she would see her son play basketball.

"That was a pretty emotional night for David," said Wade. "This was his final high school game, at the Civic Center, in front of this huge crowd. And his mother was there in a wheelchair, watching him play. He really wanted to play well for her. You could tell that the game had so much importance to him."

"Gate's mom being there was emotional for all of us," said Keith Wallace. "Dave and I started playing basketball together in the neighborhood, before I convinced him to come with me to the Cecil Kirk Rec Center to try out for the team when we were just kids. When we saw his mom there, sitting in her wheelchair, with that look of surprise and wonder on her face, the pride she had while looking at her baby, it was a special moment for every player on the team."

"I had been trying to get my mother to come to my games

for years, but she just wasn't up to it," said Wingate. "When I looked up in that crowd and saw her sitting there in her wheelchair, I nearly broke down and started crying. My brothers and sisters would always tell her how good I was, but she'd never seen me play. They finally convinced her to come, telling her that it was my last high school game before I went away to college. She would always make sure I had bus fare to get down to places like Cecil Kirk or Lafayette for practices and games. And she knew that those were some very dangerous areas. But she knew that basketball was a positive thing in my life that kept me away from the things that she wanted me to avoid. When I saw the look on her face at the beginning of that game, she looked so proud, like she felt like all of the sacrifices she made, how hard she was on me, that all of that stuff was worth it. I tried to play it cool, but on the inside, I was really emotional."

Lake Clifton was successful in keeping the game at a slow pace during the first quarter. At the end of the first eight minutes, the score was tied, 11–11. Wingate, though, had one of his worst offensive performances of the season early on.

"You could tell that David was pressing," said Wade. "With his mom being there, and the magnitude of her seeing him play for the first time, it was almost like it overwhelmed him. He was trying to do too much, trying too hard, instead of just letting the natural flow of the game come to him."

In the second quarter, the Poet offense started to click, thanks to the prolific outside shooting of Gary Graham. The Lakers focused their efforts on packing the paint and limiting what Reggie Williams and Tim Dawson could do near the basket. With Wingate missing most of his outside shots in the first quarter, Lake Clifton hung around. But Graham picked up the slack before halftime, connecting on 4 straight long-distance shots. Dunbar converted 8 of their 9 shots in the second quarter and raced out to a 31–21 halftime lead.

The Lakers would never get any closer. Leading by 23 points in the second half, Wade emptied his bench. He sent in substitutes one by one, and as each starter came out of the game, the crowd roared. Graham paced the Poets with 16 points. Dunbar was also led by Bogues in the scoring column for the first time all year, as he also scored 16 points. He took advantage of Lake Clifton's man-to-man defense all afternoon, penetrating into the lane and drawing the defense before sending some beautiful passes toward his streaking teammates. Lake Clifton decided to foul him as he began to drive the lane with ease. But Bogues made all of his free-throw attempts. He also finished with 8 assists and a plethora of steals.

"Hey, short man, congratulations," said Wade, as Muggsy sat down on the bench after receiving a standing ovation once he'd been pulled from the game in the second half. "You hit all ten of your free throws. Were they letting you shoot with a girl's ball or something?"

Bogues smiled at his coach, gave him a hug, and said, "C'mon, Coach, you know I don't miss my free throws."

"Yeah, but you still ain't take no damn charge, though," Wade said through a beaming smile.

"He's too short to take a charge, Coach, they'll just jump over his head," Reggie Williams chimed in.

"I never took a charge because I was always stealing the ball," Bogues replied. "You ain't gotta take no charge if they don't have the ball."

"And you never took a charge, either, Russ," said Wade, shooting a feigned stern look at Reggie Williams.

"That's because I blocked all those shots," Williams said playfully. "Why would I take a charge when I can just block some-body's shot? Shoot, me and Muggsy ain't takin' no damn charges."

The bench bent over in laughter. Wade turned his attention back to the substitutes in the game, barking instructions.

"All season long, the attention has gone to Williams, Wingate, and Bogues," Wade said after the game. "But Gary Graham has been our unsung hero. All year, he's been picking others up. If someone was having an off day, Gary would be the one that took up the slack. He's been our catalyst."

Reggie Williams scored 14 points and also led the Poets with 11 rebounds in the victory. Dawson scored 10 and grabbed 9 rebounds as well. Wingate, after his poor first half, showed his mother after halftime why he was one of the top players in the country. He finished with 10 points and drew gasps from the crowd as he speedily raced down the court and rocketed above the rim to block shots and dunk the ball.

After the game, Wade was asked if the rumors that Dunbar was scheduling additional games outside of competition were true. Many were saying that he'd already lined up some opponents to keep the team sharp until late March when they might play Calvert Hall to settle the question of who was the true national champion.

"I told people all along that we'd wait two weeks, but not a month," said Wade. "In my mind, the game was dead because I knew they wouldn't do it. They had everything to lose and noth-ing to gain by playing us. They did it the year before, so what was the problem now? I'll tell you what the problem was. Muggsy was the problem. They wanted no part of him."

"A lot of people call it the greatest game never played, but the way we destroyed Camden, to me, nullifies all of that debate," said Bogues. "People still argue about it and get emotional, but you can't debate the facts. Calvert Hall ducked us. So the only thing we could do was compare what happened when we both played a team that was considered one of the country's best. Camden was our common opponent, a true measuring stick if there ever was one. They struggled to beat Camden, on a neutral court. And we killed them, in their own gym, where they hadn't lost in years. So that was more important to us than the fact that we didn't play Calvert Hall."

When Wingate walked into his house after his final high school game, his mother grabbed him immediately and held him.

"She hugged me as hard as she could, sitting in that wheelchair," said Wingate. "She kept saying, over and over, how proud she was of me. She had so many struggles, especially physically, and it made me feel so good to know that I brought her some joy, that I was able to make her smile, that she was able to see that her baby was doing good. I was so happy. But at the same time, I was already feeling a little bit sad. I'd played my last game at Dunbar. I was getting ready to go out into the world. Everything was going to change. It was exciting on one hand but sad, too, because I was going to miss my boys. I was not only going to be leaving my biological family, I was also going to be leaving Mr. Wade and all of my brothers from the Dunbar family."

"We were sad to see the seniors go," said Bogues. "We had so much fun playing with them. We elevated Dunbar basketball together to a place that it had never been before, and that was in the discussion for a national championship. So me, Reggie Williams, Tim Dawson, and Reggie Lewis, we went back to the rec centers. We were working out, getting ready for the summer tournaments and the national camps like Five-Star, where we'd go head-to-head with the other top players in the country."

"At the end of the season, I was already looking forward to

the next year," said Reggie Williams. "I was looking forward to taking my college visits and getting one step closer to my dream. I told Muggsy that we were going to go undefeated again and win that national championship."

"We knew we'd have some new guys coming in the next year who would be really good," said Bogues. "We knew that Mr. Wade was going to have us playing a national schedule the next year. We were going to take that Poetry in Motion out on the road. So from the day of that last game in 1982 at the Civic Center, we made a pact with one another. We all agreed that the next year, there wasn't going to be any debate about who the best team in the country was. We were going to go undefeated again. We weren't going to leave any doubts. And anything other than achieving our goal of delivering Dunbar a national championship was not going to be acceptable.

"Before my junior year at Dunbar, basketball had been a hobby," said Bogues. "It was something that we all loved to do. But after that season, it became more than that. I started to realize that the guys we looked up to like Skip Wise and Ernie Graham, they were talented enough to take the game as far as they wanted. But drugs took them off the path. My dad being involved in a criminal lifestyle took him off his path of being a father who could be there for us whenever we needed him. I walked into the season just wanting to play ball with my boys, but I walked out of it with a vision.

"Me and Russ made a pact, that we were going to stay on the right path, that we were going to overcome all of the obstacles, distractions, and negative influences. That was the first time I felt the true power of that orange ball. It not only gave me so many wonderful role models and friendships, it taught me about values, principles, integrity, work ethic, having a positive attitude, hard work, and being a leader. And, like Mr. Wade always said, regardless of all the success we might find on the court, it was what we did off the court that was really going to matter. It's hard to describe, but after that season, it was like everything fell into place. I had this vision. And nothing was going to stop me. When I got to Dunbar, I was just a young kid. After that season, I felt like a young man, a young man who was ready to chase his dream."

CHAPTER THIRTEEN

"The Greatest Peanut Since Planters!"

DURING THE SUMMER OF 1982, Bob Wade drove a van to the prestigious Five-Star Basketball Camp, which was being held at Robert Morris University in Moon Township, Pennsylvania. Reggie Williams had made a name for himself during the previous summer at Five-Star, where the country's best players and top college and prep coaches gathered for a number of one-week sessions of drills, instruction, and competitive league play. In addition to Williams, who was now considered the top high school player in the country as he entered his senior year, Wade brought most of his team's returning players, along with some who would be transferring to Dunbar in the fall like Herman "Tree" Harried, who had previously attended Eastern High School, and Mike Brown, who was coming in from Cardinal Gibbons.

When the camp's director, Howard Garfinkel, greeted Wade upon his arrival and saw the surplus of long-limbed players climbing out of the van, Garfinkel hugged him, called him by the nick-name that he was fond of using for him, and said, "Sugar, I see you've been keeping a lot of secrets up there in Baltimore."

But he would soon find out that the biggest secret of all was the shortest player in the camp.

"When I left the camp in 2008, after starting it in 1966, we had over three hundred and fifty campers who went on to play in the NBA," said Garfinkel. "We had two hundred eighty-eight counselors and high school coaches who went on to coach major college basketball. We had thirty-two of those guys who went on to become NBA coaches. Five-Star was the training ground for the best of the best. And Sugar Wade was awesome. He was one of the great high school coaches who would come to Five-Star every summer, bringing some of the best players from Baltimore with him over the years. He was an outstanding coach and teacher. He really cared about those kids."

While the players were participating in workouts and drills, Garfinkel and his staff would evaluate and rank them individu-ally. The country's best players, who attended for free and worked as waiters in the dining hall, were assigned to the "NBA division." The camp would hold a dispersal draft to place players on differ-ent teams, which would compete against one another to deter-mine the champion.

"We would always start the draft with centers," said Garfin-kel. "There were twelve teams in the league, and Wade, after all the coaches picked out of a hat, was designated with the last pick in the first round, which meant that he got the worst center. We'd pick point guards next, which meant that he had the first pick at that position and could choose the best playmaker in the camp to run his team."

When Wade picked Muggsy Bogues as his point guard, Gar-finkel became irate.

"There were so many great players there that week," said Garfinkel. "There were at least six big-name, top-notch point guards who would go on to be stars in college basketball. I normally just observed the draft and never intervened, but when Wade picked Muggsy, I said, 'Hey! Whoa! Stop! I void this pick. You can't do this, Sugar. You have to take one of the top guards.' I didn't know who Muggsy was at the time, other than that he was Wade's point guard at Dunbar. I'd seen him in drills but hadn't yet seen him play in an organized game situation. Reggie Williams was the big name from that Dunbar crew. I'd never heard of Muggsy. He was five foot three and wasn't ranked anywhere near where some of the top guys with the big names were ranked."

Wade insisted, and an intense argument ensued, leading to him and Garfinkel having to be separated.

"I told Garf that not only was I drafting Muggsy as my point guard, but I intended to use him as my horse," said Wade. "At Five-Star, you had to play all of the players at least half the game. But you could designate one guy as the team's horse, and you could play him as much as possible. Most coaches used guys like Patrick Ewing, Ralph Sampson, and Len Bias, the big superstar players, as their horses. When he heard that, he became even angrier."

"We were yelling back and forth at each other, and I screamed, 'You can't do that! You've got the worst center. Now you've got a chance to take the best point guard in the country and you're taking this kid Muggsy? You're screwing up the entire camp and the whole league!' " said Garfinkel.

The argument escalated with Garfinkel adamant that he was voiding the selection.

"He told me that I was killing the league, that my team was dead, and that the whole league was dead," said Wade. "Garf said with the worst center and Muggsy as our point guard, that we'd never win a game. But I didn't budge. It got heated for a moment and we cursed each other out. Finally, I told him, 'Look, I can get the hell out of here right now and take all of my players with me. I know what the hell I'm doing. If I can't take Muggsy as my point guard and my horse, I'm going home right now.'"

Garfinkel seethed but finally acquiesced.

"We almost came to blows, which would not have been good for me," said Garfinkel. "Finally, I gave up and said, 'Fine! You've got a chance to take a superstar and win some games. But have it your way. You're screwing up the whole draft and the whole league, and you won't win a single game. You wanna screw the whole camp up? Screw it. Go ahead and take him.' And I just stayed quiet for the rest of the draft."

"Being from the Washington, DC, area, I knew about Muggsy and heard about his Dunbar team, but that was the first time I had a chance to play against him, at Five-Star," said former Duke University standout point guard Tommy Amaker, now the head coach at Harvard University. "He was a terror! You definitely stayed up a little bit longer at night knowing that you had to go up against that guy the next day. You knew it was going to be a long day because he was going to be in your shirt, in your jock, he was just going to be everywhere you went, causing extreme havoc defensively. During the camp, he was stealing the ball all over the court, just embarrassing people. And offensively, he was throwing these incredible passes. He was just blowing by guys. You couldn't keep him in front of you. When I was playing against him, I kept telling myself, 'You have to be tight with the ball against this guy.' You were lucky if he didn't take the ball from you four or five times in a game."

"Muggsy tore that Five-Star camp up," said Reggie Williams. "He wasn't just good, he dominated. All of those point guards that had big names and big reputations, he destroyed all of them the same way he destroyed Kevin Walls in that Camden game. And it wasn't even close."

"My god, was I wrong," said Garfinkel. "Muggsy was the best point guard in the whole camp. Wade was right. I had to take him out to dinner. The next day after the draft, when we calmed down and were back to being buddies again, we made a bet that if he won the championship, that I would take him out to dinner. I never thought in a million years that I would lose that bet. And wouldn't you know, his team went undefeated, they won the championship, and Muggsy won the Most Valuable Player award and the Best Playmaker award. After watching him play, I realized that he was the eighth wonder of the world. He was the most incredible thing that I ever saw at Five-Star. And there's never been anything like him since."

In addition to Bogues's spectacular performance, Williams was named the MVP of the league's All-Star game for three consecutive weeks. It was a feat that Michael Jordan, Patrick Ewing, Chris Paul, Lebron James, and all of the other elite players in the camp's history never accomplished.

"We owned Five-Star that entire summer," said Herman "Tree" Harried. "We were all putting in work. All of the coaches and players kept talking about Baltimore that summer. They couldn't believe that we had so many great players. And they were really shocked that we were all on the same high school team. That was the first time that I recognized just how big Coach Wade was in terms of the respect that he had on a national level. All of the top college coaches were there, but to see how they interacted with him and the respect that he had from everybody was something else. I thought he was just 'the Man' in Baltimore. At Five-Star, I realized that he was 'the Man' all over the country, as far as basketball was concerned."

Despite Bogues's garnering the accolades, recognition, and national respect that he deserved from most of the camp's players and coaches, he was singled out one night by the camp's featured speaker—a young, rising star in the coaching fraternity.

"It was early on in the camp, and Rick Pitino, who was then the head coach at Boston University, was giving his speech," said Bogues. "And he called me out. He said he was watching some little guard at the camp throwing no-look passes behind his neck and between his legs and stuff like that. It was obvious that he was talking about me. He actually said that he was disgusted by what he saw. He said it was hot-dogging and that we weren't there to play playground ball. I was furious. He really made me mad. I might have played a fancy style, but I was always about winning and making my teammates better. He really motivated me. I didn't tone down my style, but I was even more determined to kick everybody's butt at that camp after that."

When he returned home to the Lafayette Projects after the Five-Star camp, Bogues checked his mailbox and was shocked to find a recruiting letter waiting for him from Boston University.

"I didn't even open it," said Bogues. "I just ripped it up and threw it in the trash. There was no way I was going to play at Boston University for Rick Pitino after the way that he had disrespected me."

In the "In Depth Five-Star Camp Report," the scouting analysis that Garfinkel sent to the hundreds of college coaches who subscribed to his service, he gave Bogues the highest ranking possible of five stars, which he affixed to players whom he projected to be key prospects for a nationally ranked team on the college level. In September of 1982, Garfinkel wrote: "Even Ripley wouldn't believe it! Muggsy is one of the most exciting, productive transition guards in years, a one-man fast break, a human assist—for him to be a key factor, however, you must run, run, run, while a 94-foot game will help negate his obvious size detriment on 'D' . . . perpetual motion steals offset the opposition's post-up strategy—incredible 3-on-2 and 2-on-1 playmaker aided by a large degree to indefensible passing angles that only he can create—fullback's legs never stop churning, a constant threat to the careless dribbler or dumb pivot man (he who puts it down is lost!)—THE GREATEST PEANUT SINCE PLANTERS!"

Later on that summer, Bogues and Reggie Williams were able to extract a measure of revenge against the majority of Calvert Hall's star players during the city's most prestigious and competitive summer tournament, the BNBL, the Baltimore Neighborhood Basketball League.

"The Calvert Hall coach, Amatucci, might have been able to keep his team away from us during the regular season, but he couldn't do anything about it in the summer," said Bogues. "We played for the Lafayette Rec when the school season wasn't going on, and those guys played for the Madison Square Rec. We smacked them that summer in the BNBL and won the championship. It felt good to know that we got the bragging rights, but it was still a disappointment that we didn't get to do it in front of the whole city with our high school teams during the season."

———

As the 1982–1983 high school basketball season began in Baltimore, Wade rolled out the bricks and the sandbags on the first day of practice as he gave his usual speech, saying, "There's no pill that anyone can invent that will get you into the type of shape that you need to be in."

Prior to the season tipping off, the Poets were a unanimous choice among the national publications as the number one team in the nation. Reggie Williams was widely regarded as the nation's top high school player in the class of 1983. Bogues, Williams, and Tim Dawson returned to their starting positions. Keith James, a sophomore on the previous year's team, took the place of Gary Graham as the starting shooting guard. Mike Brown, the new transfer from Cardinal Gibbons, assumed David Wingate's starting position at small forward. Although Reggie Lewis was talented enough to start, Wade elected to keep him as the team's sixth man. New transfer Herman "Tree" Harried was another devastating weapon coming off the Dunbar bench.

"Truck and Tree could have easily started for us, but when they came into the game, we became an even stronger, more dangerous team," said Wade. "Truck wasn't necessarily pleased with that decision, but he worked his butt off and never complained."

The Poets wasted no time in making a statement that next season against some powerful competition.

In early December, at the Beltway Classic tournament at Towson University, the Poets tested themselves against another highly ranked team, Coach Morgan Wootten's DeMatha Catholic squad, which featured one of the country's top and most highly recruited big men, Danny Ferry. The Poets were scheduled to meet at Dunbar at 6:00 p.m. before they boarded the bus for the short ride over to Towson. As Bogues walked toward the school entrance, he ran into the team's cheerleaders, whose coach told him that Wade and his teammates had already left.

"I was like, Coach Wade told us to be here by six o'clock and I'm right on time. There's no way that he left me," said Bogues. "I ran into the gym, where we normally met, and it was empty; the lights were out. I couldn't believe it. I was thinking, 'How is Coach Wade gonna leave early without me?' I was upset. The cheerleading coach said I could catch a ride with them, so that's what I did.

And that was actually a lot of fun. But when I got to the arena, the team wasn't there. So I just waited for them to get there."

Wade was waiting as well, but he was still in East Baltimore. The team, which normally met in the gym, assembled in the locker room that night, an instruction that Muggsy had forgotten. A stickler for detail who always stressed being on time, Wade constantly told his team that if any player was ever late, the team would leave without him and he wouldn't be able to play.

"But he was waiting for me on that night, and Reggie and the rest of the guys were getting a big kick out of that," said Bogues.

"Coach Wade was always barking that stuff about being late and getting left, but there was no way that he was leaving Muggsy," said Williams. "We didn't let him see it, but we were all laughing about that one. We knew that we weren't going to play our biggest game of the year without the little fella. But when he never showed up, we started getting nervous because that just wasn't like Muggsy. We knew that something must have happened."

Wade sent Marshall Goodwin over to Bogues's apartment; he rode over there in his sheriff's vehicle with the siren blazing and lights flashing.

"My mom said when Marshall pulled up, everybody thought it was a raid or something," said Bogues. "She told him that I'd already left a while ago to head over to the school."

Wade instructed the bus driver to drive into the projects, and the players fanned out, asking everyone they knew if they'd seen or heard from Muggsy.

"They went to the rec center, knocked on people's doors, and no one knew where I was," said Bogues.

"It got to the point where we had no choice but to leave and head over to the game," said Wade. "As we pulled onto the Towson campus, I wondered if somebody had actually kidnapped him. He had been late to practice once the previous year, because he was getting a haircut and lost track of time. But other than that, Muggsy was dependable. I had all types of bad thoughts running through my mind in terms of what might have happened to him. His mom told Marshall that he left for the gym, but he never showed up. I was just hoping that he was okay."

As the team disembarked and began walking toward the arena, one of the players spotted Bogues standing outside and yelled, "Hey, there goes Muggs!"

"I was relieved to see his little behind standing out there," said Wade. "But now that I knew that he was okay, I became angry. I should have been calm, hugged him, and told him how happy I was to see him. But I started yelling at him."

"Coach Wade was hollering at me, screaming, 'Boy, where the hell were you? I ought to take my fist and go right upside your little head,'" said Bogues.

When Wade questioned his commitment to the team, Bogues began yelling back. He explained that the cheerleading coach told him that the team had already left, that he ran into the gym and that all of the lights were out, that the entire situation wasn't his fault. The yelling escalated until Edgar Lee Bell, the man who had mentored and coached Wade while he was in middle school, intervened.

"Bobby!" yelled Mr. Lee. "Punish him after the game. He's here now, so let's go inside and just win the damn game."

"I was so mad, I was crying and yelling at Coach Wade, telling him that I wasn't going to play," said Bogues. "He yelled right back, 'Get your little butt inside and get your clothes on.'"

In the locker room, Muggsy was still animated, yelling, "He didn't have to yell at me like that, it wasn't my fault, you guys all know that I'm always gonna be there for you."

Reggie Williams walked over to his buddy, put his arm around his shoulders, and said, "Hey, Little Fella, to hell with him, man. Forget about it. Let's go kick DeMatha's ass."

Bogues still had tears in his eyes as the team prepared to take the floor for their warm-ups. His mother and his sister, Sherron, came over to calm him down and wipe the tears from his cheeks.

A few moments before the game started, Wade walked up to his point guard and apologized. "Hey, Short Man, I'm sorry," he said. "I was scared that something had happened to you when you didn't show up. I should have hugged you instead of screaming at you. There's a lot of people in here that came to see us put on a show today. Are you all right? Are you ready to play some Poet basketball?"

"Yeah, I'm fine," Bogues said, though he was clearly still angry. "Let's do it."

The Poets didn't disappoint, defeating DeMatha by 12 points and Archbishop Carroll the next day by 20 to capture the Beltway Classic championship. During the DeMatha game, there was one sequence that is still talked about in the high school gyms and on the playgrounds of Baltimore to this day. After one of his steals, Muggsy motored toward the hoop in full attack mode. He jumped high toward the rim as DeMatha's big men converged on him in midflight. Just when it looked like he was going to get his shot blocked, he did a 360-degree spin in midair and flipped an alley-oop pass behind his neck that Reggie Williams caught while soaring to the rim. Williams threw down a monster dunk that caused fans to spill out of the stands momentarily.

"I couldn't do that move again if I tried," said Bogues. "I was still angry, the adrenaline was flowing, the crowd was going crazy, and me and Reggie had that incredible chemistry. He didn't know what I was going to do with the ball, because I didn't know, either. But he knew to attack the rim because I was going to find some way to get him the ball."

DeMatha's coach, Morgan Wootten, an authority on high school basketball if there ever was one, had competed against Skip Wise's great Dunbar team in 1973 and the phenomenal Lew Alcindor's Power Memorial team in 1965, among many others. After the game, Wootten said, "Dunbar is as fine a high school team as I have ever seen. I've never seen one better. The thing that Dunbar has that none of those other teams had is Bogues."

Over the Christmas holiday, Wade opted to play in a very competitive tournament in Johnstown, Pennsylvania. The Johnstown trip was a coming-out party for the team's sixth man, Reggie Lewis. Against a talented field of competitors, Lewis dazzled throughout the tournament while getting extensive playing time. He was eventually named the event's Most Valuable Player.

"We all knew what he could do because we saw it every day in practice, but Truck's performance in Johnstown let the cat out of the bag," said Wade. "He was phenomenal. Our starters got into foul trouble throughout that tournament, with the exception of Muggsy. And Truck showed that he could handle the ball on the perimeter, that he was a natural scorer who could get points in the paint and out on the wing. Jim Calhoun, the coach at Northeastern University, who was recruiting him the hardest, got really nervous after Johnstown. He knew that after that performance, the big schools were going to try to get in at the last minute on his recruitment."

"We were all excited for Truck when he won the MVP award," said Bogues. "He saved us because when Russ and Tim Dawson got in foul trouble up in Johnstown, he came off the bench, played big minutes, and performed like he was the best player in the country. He was really showing off up there, displaying his entire repertoire. We already knew he was special, but he opened a lot of eyes with his performance up there. He would show glimpses in the limited playing time that he got, coming off the bench. But in that tournament, he showed all of those college scouts who were in the stands just how special of a player he really was."

Back at the hotel later that evening, after his MVP performance, Lewis declined Muggsy's invitation to sneak out of the hotel to hang out with some girls they had met during the tournament.

"I got back to the hotel after having dinner with my wife and the tournament promoters and noticed that the hallways were too quiet," said Wade. "I started knocking on doors and everybody was gone. OJ had sprained his ankle during the tournament, and I found him hanging out with Reggie Williams, who never went anywhere, in Mr. Badham's room. They said they didn't know where the other guys had gone. The only other guys who stayed at the hotel were Truck and one of the new reserves on the team, Reggie McNeil. Truck said he didn't know where the other guys were. I applied some pressure to Reggie McNeil, and he told me that Muggsy had met some girls and rounded everybody up to go to a party with them."

When Wade asked Lewis why he didn't go to the party, he said, "Mr. Wade, I just didn't feel like going. Plus, I won the MVP tonight, and I didn't want to do anything to get on your bad side."

Wade dispatched Marshall Goodwin to track the boys down. The teenage party was at a local community center not far from the hotel. Despite having to trudge through some piercingly frigid weather in unfamiliar territory, it didn't take long for Goodwin to find it. When he walked in, at the center of the dance floor, he found Bogues, who was dancing up a storm.

"Marshall came in and walked right up to me," said Bogues. "I was getting my boogie on! I knew we were busted and there was no excuse that I could make. So I just smiled at him, called him the nickname that we had for him, and kept dancing. I said, 'Hey, Hammer Head, I see you out on the dance floor. Show me what you got.' He just looked at me and shook his head and said, 'Boy, round everybody up and get your little ass outta here.' We did a whole lot of extra running with those bricks when we got back to Baltimore. But it was worth it. We had a ball up there. And Truck winning the MVP made it that much sweeter."

The Poets won the prestigious King of the Bluegrass Tournament in Kentucky against top-notch competition, destroying all of their opponents. They finished the season undefeated again, 31–0, and were named as the consensus national champions of high school baskeball.

Once again Calvert Hall would not schedule a game against Dunbar. Not until the 1983–84 season, after Wingate, Williams, Lewis, and Bogues had all graduated, would Calvert Hall play Dunbar. Keith James, Herman Harried, and Mike Brown were now the big stars at Dunbar. Duane Ferrell was a senior for Calvert Hall that year. The game was played in front of a packed house at Baltimore's Civic Center. Dunbar won the game handily.

"During the '81–'82 and '82–'83 seasons, I knew that those teams were very special," said Wade. "As the years progressed and the more that I thought about it and reflected back on those experiences, I realized that they were probably the best high school teams that were ever assembled. We worked our tails off and took care of business. We beat some great teams and blew out some really good ones. But the thing that stands out was the love that we had for one another and the laughs that we shared."

EPILOGUE

IN LATE APRIL 2015, as images of the unrest in Baltimore were featured on newscasts across the country due to the death of Freddie Gray, a twenty-five-year-old resident of West Baltimore, while in police custody, Muggsy Bogues watched with tears in his eyes.

He jumped in his car and drove from Charlotte, North Carolina, calling friends and family members, asking them where he could go to help out. His city was in pain, he was hurting. His home, the place that had made him who he was, that provided his greatest life lessons, was in turmoil with some 350 businesses damaged and looted, sixty buildings and 150 motor vehicles set on fire, 250 people arrested, and a state of emergency declared as National Guard troops were deployed.

Without any fanfare or media spotlight, he blended into the crowd to protest, to shout, to offer young people and the communities that he loved some support and hope.

SKIP WISE was in and out of prison in the 1970s and '80s but eventually overcame his drug addiction and distanced himself from his drug-dealing past. Today, he counsels and mentors adolescents in Baltimore's residential group home facilities. He is still considered the best basketball player that Baltimore has ever produced.

———

Beset by disrepair, high rates of crime, rampant gunfire, and an out-of-control narcotics trade, the Lafayette Courts housing projects were demolished in 1995. In 1997, a new housing development of attached town houses called Pleasant View Gardens opened on the site.

JULIA WOODLAND, Dunbar's former principal, who had worked for over forty years as an educator in Baltimore, passed away at Maryland General Hospital in 1998. She was seventy years old.

LEON HOWARD, the former director of the Lafayette Recreation Center, who many say helped to rewrite the city's basketball history, still lives in Baltimore. He retired from the Baltimore City Department of Recreation and Parks in 2002. He spends a lot of his free time today swimming and exercising. Seventy-six years old, he rarely attends any high school basketball games anymore. He speaks with his former protégés Reggie Williams and Muggsy Bogues regularly. They still call him Fat Man.

ANTHONY "DUDIE" LEWIS retired as the director of the Cecil Kirk Recreation Center in 2012. He's still in charge of Cecil Kirk's basketball program. His most recent mentee to become an NBA star is the Sacramento Kings' Rudy Gay.

ERNIE GRAHAM turned his life around and got sober in 1995. He started a nonprofit program called Get the Message, which established after-school programs and support services for area youth, securing grant money from, among others, Baltimore Ravens' owner Steve Bisciotti and Baltimore Orioles' legend Cal Ripken. He owns commercial and residential real estate in his old neighborhood.

HOWARD GARFINKEL, the founder of the Five-Star Basketball Camp, was inducted into the Naismith Memorial Basketball Hall of Fame in 2014. Almost ninety years old, Garfinkel lives in New York City and can still be seen attending some of the elite high school basketball events throughout the country.

WILLIAM "SUGAR" CAIN, considered the "Father of Dunbar Basketball," and who coached for thirty-two years at the school, died of cancer at the age of eighty in his West Baltimore home. "He passed the baton to me, and all I tried to do was continue his legacy and values," Bob Wade told the *Baltimore Sun* when Cain passed away. "He demanded respect and discipline and was a father figure not only to me but to many kids from single-parent families."

KEITH JAMES, the lone sophomore reserve on the '81–'82 Poets, played his college basketball at the University of South Carolina and at the University of Nevada at Las Vegas. After college, he received his real estate license and settled in Nevada.

KEITH WALLACE attended the State Police Academy after graduating from Dunbar. He dropped out within a few months and enrolled at the Community College of Baltimore County in Essex, Maryland, where he started for the basketball team. He currently lives in Maryland and works in the computer networking and information systems technology field.

DARRYL "OJ" WOOD accepted a basketball scholarship to Virginia State University. He left school after two years to enlist in the Marine Corps. He retired after a twenty-year career in the military and is currently a civilian Marine Corps employee who specializes in audiovisual technology.

JERRY WHITE attended Morgan State University after Dunbar and did not play basketball in college. He eventually left school and enlisted in the Air Force. He went back to college in 2010 and earned his bachelor's degree in computer science from the University of Baltimore in May of 2014. He is currently the information technology manager at the Baltimore nonprofit agency People Encouraging People.

ERIC GREEN earned a football scholarship to James Madison University in Virginia, where he was an accomplished four-year starting quarterback. He was invited to a number of NFL minicamps, where teams gave him a tryout as a defensive back. When pro football didn't materialize, he began working as a corrections officer in the Baltimore city jail. In 1996, he joined the Baltimore City Police Department. He is currently a detective in the investigation and intelligence division.

TIM DAWSON began his college basketball career at George Washington University in Washington, DC, where he was named to the Atlantic 10 All-Rookie Team as a freshman, before transferring to play his final three years at the University of Miami. He went on to receive a PhD in education and was a high school principal at Killian Senior High School in Miami, City College High School in Baltimore, and South Hagerstown High School in Hagerstown, Maryland. Now retired, he and his wife, who is a physician, own and operate residential assisted-living facilities for the elderly in Maryland.

GARY GRAHAM played at the University of Nevada at Las Vegas and was a captain on the 1987 Runnin' Rebels Final Four team that went 37–2. He played professional basketball overseas for six years and worked as an executive in the casino business for a number of years after returning to Las Vegas.

DAVID "GATE" WINGATE was a starter and key contributor on Georgetown University's national championship team in 1984. Selected in the second round of the 1986 draft by the Philadelphia 76ers, he played for a number of teams during his fifteen-year NBA career.

REGGIE LEWIS went on to become the all-time leading scorer at Northeastern University. He was picked by the Boston Celtics in the first round of the 1987 NBA draft. He blossomed into an excellent professional player and was named an NBA All-Star in 1992. He also became a team captain of the venerable Celtics franchise. Ironically, many people believe that Lewis, who wasn't a starter on his Dunbar teams, became the best NBA player to come out of Dunbar. Sadly, he died at the age of twenty-seven in 1993, while shooting baskets at the Celtics' practice facility. The cause of death was attributed to hypertrophic cardiomyopathy, a structural heart defect.

As the *New York Times* reported on September 13, 1993, "Boston Celtics star Reggie Lewis, who collapsed and died on July 27, reportedly was born with a heart murmur and came from a family with a history of cardiac illness."

Autopsy results revealed that Lewis had a large, extensively scarred heart. He'd apparently not mentioned to the doctors who treated him for dizzy spells and an earlier collapse that his younger brother was born with a hole in his heart and had undergone open-heart surgery at the age of four, or that his mother had had two heart attacks, one when she was just a teenager. The speculation was that he hid his family history, along with his own heart murmur as a child, because he did not want to be forced to retire from playing the game that he loved.

REGGIE "RUSS" WILLIAMS was named a McDonald's All-American after his final season at Dunbar in 1983. As a freshman at Georgetown University, he scored 19 points and collected 7 rebounds in the Hoyas national title game victory over the University of Houston, playing alongside David Wingate. Along with Patrick Ewing, Alonzo Mourning, and Allen Iverson, he is considered one of the greatest players in Georgetown basketball history. Selected as the fourth overall pick in the 1987 draft by the Los Angeles Clippers, Williams played ten years in the NBA before a knee injury ended his career. Williams has held numerous head coaching positions on the high school and community college level in recent years. Williams currently owns the Shooting Stars Basketball Academy in Bowie, Maryland, which offers individualized basketball training, after-school programs, skills clinics, tournaments, summer camps, tutoring, academic enrichment, and college preparatory services.

TYRONE "MUGGSY" BOGUES received scholarship offers from more than a dozen colleges and chose to attend Wake Forest University.

As a freshman at Wake Forest, he came off the bench in short spurts and didn't receive much playing time. After being inserted into the starting lineup at the beginning of his sophomore year,

Bogues proved his worth. In the Demon Deacons' 91–89 upset victory over Duke, which was ranked as the country's number two team in the college basketball polls at the time, Bogues held Johnny Dawkins, the Blue Devils' prolific scoring machine and All-American, to 8 points, while the fans in Cameron Indoor Stadium repeatedly taunted him by screaming, "Stand up!" It was the first time in his fifty-two college games that Dawkins did not score in double figures.

Two weeks after Wake Forest's stunning upset against Duke during his sophomore year, Bogues scored 20 points and collected 10 assists and 4 steals against North Carolina State, as television commentator and former national championship coach Al McGuire gushed, "I've never seen a player dominate the game the way he did."

Perhaps the greatest sign of respect came from the notorious Duke fans at Cameron Indoor Stadium, when they gave him a standing ovation after a 12-assist and 6-steal performance during his junior year. Bogues led the Atlantic Coast Conference in steals and assists for three consecutive years. He finished his college career as the ACC's career leader in both categories. During his senior year at Wake Forest, he proved that he could also score, when he averaged 15 points per game.

NBA scouts began to take serious notice of his rare talent during the 1986 FIBA World Championships in Madrid. Playing alongside Duke's Amakar, North Carolina's Kenny Smith, the Naval Academy's David Robinson, and Arizona's Steve Kerr and Sean Elliott, among others on the talented roster, Bogues dazzled on the international stage. In the second round of the tournament, he held Yugoslavia's 6-foot-6 star player Drazen Petrovic, who was averaging over 26 points in his nine previous tournament games, to 12.

Bogues led the United States team with 10 steals and 5 assists in their thrilling 87–85 victory over the Soviet Union in the championship game. He became such a crowd favorite that the Spanish press affectionately dubbed him "La Chispa Negra" (the Black Spark). One writer for the Spanish newspaper *El Pais* wrote, "He has nerves of steel and super-flexible muscles. On the court he appears to be a little brother of his teammates, but it is he who orders, commands, and directs."

The 1986 USA World Championship basketball team was the last unit comprised solely of college players that would win a gold medal in the Olympics or World Championships. John Thompson, the famed coach at Georgetown University, who had recruited David Wingate and Reggie Williams from Dunbar and had won a national championship with them, said the biggest mistake he'd ever made as a college coach was not recruiting Bogues.

Muggsy was drafted with the twelfth overall pick in the first round of the 1987 NBA draft. He enjoyed a fourteen-year career in the NBA with four teams, most notably the Charlotte Hornets. He is still the franchise's career leader in minutes played, assists, and steals. To this day, he remains the most beloved player in Hornets history. At 5 foot 3, he is the shortest player ever to play in the NBA.

Bogues was introduced to a new generation of fans when he appeared with Michael Jordan in the 1996 Warner Bros. movie *Space Jam*. He lives in the Charlotte area and has served as the head coach of the WNBA's Charlotte Sting and at United Faith Christian Academy, a private high school. He currently works as a special ambassador with the Hornets and as a global ambassador with the NBA, teaching basketball clinics and spreading the gospel of the league.

BOB WADE, after compiling a record of 341 wins and 24 losses over his ten-year career at Dunbar High School, which included four perfect seasons, nine Maryland Scholastic Association "A" Conference titles, and two national championships, was offered the head coaching position at the University of Maryland in October of 1986 at the age of forty-one. He was hired to replace Maryland's former coach of seventeen years, Lefty Driesell, in the wake of a scandal that surfaced at the school as a result of star player and All-American Len Bias's drug overdose and death.

With his background as a tough disciplinarian who stressed academics, along with his accomplished coaching résumé, he was tasked with cleaning up the program, despite the fact that he did not have any experience at the college level. Wade became the first African American coach of a major sport in the history of the Atlantic Coast Conference.

Unable to recruit any new players for his inaugural season at Maryland and with player suspensions and defections as a result of the Len Bias tragedy, Wade's Terrapins did not win a game in the ACC, going 0–14 in conference and finishing with an overall record of 9–17 during the 1986–1987 season. But after Wade brought in his first recruiting class, the Terps rebounded and Maryland was once again an NCAA Tournament team.

"I brought the bricks with me to Maryland, and the players were not accustomed to the drills and the practice regimen that I used," said Wade. "They whispered among themselves, 'Oh, he's just a high school coach, he doesn't know the college game, you don't do these types of things on the college level.' Well, after that first year when I couldn't recruit, the next year we went to the NCAA Tournament, so all that talk stopped."

The player/coach dynamic at Maryland was significantly different as well. At Dunbar, he was an almost mythical figure who was revered and had known most of his players' families before the players were even born.

"At Dunbar it was, 'Mr. Wade said to do it that way, so we're gonna do it that way as best we can,' and there wasn't any questioning out loud of why," said Wade. "But at Maryland, there was some eye-rolling and negative feedback." When two key players transferred out in Wade's third season, the team regressed and lost twenty games. Wade was forced to resign in May of 1989 after compiling a record of 36–50 over his three years. In only two years of recruiting, he managed to sign three future first-round NBA draft picks in Brian Williams (who later changed his name to Bison Dele), Walt Williams, and Jerrod Mustaf.

Wade's forced resignation coincided with allegations that he committed NCAA infractions during his short stint at Maryland. The infractions report issued by the NCAA in March of 1990 cited "major violations of NCAA legislation" and a "lack of institutional control." Those words ended Wade's career as a college coach. The university was placed on probation and punished more severely for the infractions that took place under Wade's watch than for the drug and academic scandal that he had been brought in to remediate.

"I spent my whole life building my reputation, and the way things happened at Maryland, they were trying to destroy my credibility," said Wade. "I knew nothing about two of Lefty's former assistant coaches that I was forced to retain, [who] were doing the same things that they had been doing when Lefty was there. They'd take recruits to a store on Route 1 called Terp territory, where the kid would pick out hundreds of dollars' worth of merchandise and then pay the owner, who was a Maryland booster, one dollar. I didn't know anything about that, but those coaches and that booster lied to the NCAA and said I directed it, but that had been going on long before I got to Maryland."

Wade insists that he never directed his staff to be dishonest with the NCAA investigators.

"I invited all of the coaches over to my house to go through the entire situation because I wanted to get to the bottom of everything," said Wade. "I wanted to know what happened and who was responsible for what. The only guys who showed up were Woody Williams, the former Lake Clifton coach whom I brought with me to Maryland, and Jeff Adkins. Adkins was the only coach who'd previously worked under Lefty who supported the changes I was trying to make to a program that was filthy."

Adkins admitted that he took part in a ticket-selling scheme where the proceeds were given to the players, but said that it had been a common practice in the program dating back many years.

"The way it came out, it looks like I was the first person ever to do that, but it was like a tradition at Maryland," Adkins, a former Terp who'd played under Lefty Driesell as well, told the *Baltimore Sun*'s Don Markus in 1989. "It was a tradition in the ACC (for the tournament). Some good people sold their tickets."

When asked to respond to Adkins's statement, Driesell said he was unaware of any ticket-selling scheme during his sixteen years as Maryland's coach.

Bob Wade never coached again. In the summer of 2015, he retired from his long-held position as the director of athletics for the Baltimore City Public Schools system. On Tuesday, January 6, 2015, before the Poets played Edmondson High School, the Baltimore City School Board honored him by naming the basketball court at Dunbar High School "Coach Wade Court." Ostensibly, the ceremony paid homage to his accomplishments during his eleven years as the school's head coach, his overall record of 272–24 while leading the program to national prominence, the nine Maryland Scholastic Association "A" Conference titles, the four undefeated seasons, and the two national championships. But his accomplishments and impact went much further than wins, losses, and championships. Many of his former players returned to the school to hug their former coach and thank him for what he meant in their lives.

Bob Wade, during his tenure at Dunbar, helped more than two hundred student-athletes whom he coached in football and basketball receive college scholarships. In addition to the current Dunbar students who were waiting for the game to begin, a large contingent of elderly people sat in the gym, fondly recalling the powerhouse days of the early 1980s and what those teams meant to a struggling community.

Muggsy Bogues traveled from North Carolina to be there.

"There are so many things you can say about Coach," Bogues said during the ceremony. "He affected so many of our lives. It was such a pleasure knowing that he was a guy who had your back, who had your best interests at heart. He taught us so many things beyond basketball. He gave us that focus, that willingness, that attitude, that determination to want to be more than just an athlete. We didn't just strive to simply be the best basketball player. We wanted to become the best person, the best family man, and that's what Coach did for us."

He then looked at Wade, with his eyes beginning to water, and said, "Coach, you know what you mean to me. You believed in me, and that's why I was able to accomplish the things that I was able to accomplish. No one, no one can understand how important you were to us."

APPENDIX: CAREER STATISTICS, COLLEGE AND NBA, PER GAME AVERAGE

Muggsy Bogues Career Stats, Per Game

COLLEGE

YEARS	TEAM	REBOUNDS	ASSISTS	STEALS	POINTS
4	Wake Forest	2.4	6.6	2.3	8.3

NBA

GAMES	TEAM	REBOUNDS	ASSISTS	STEALS	POINTS
632	Charlotte	2.6	8.8	1.7	8.8
95	Golden State	2.1	4.9	1.1	5.5
83	Toronto	1.7	3.7	0.8	4.9
79	Washington	1.7	5.1	1.6	5.0

Reggie Lewis Career Stats, Per Game

COLLEGE

YEARS	TEAM	REBOUNDS	ASSISTS	STEALS	POINTS
4	Northeastern	7.9	1.7	1.9	22.2

NBA

GAMES	TEAM	REBOUNDS	ASSISTS	STEALS	POINTS
450	Boston	4.6	2.3	1.3	17.6

Reggie Williams Career Stats, Per Game

COLLEGE

YEARS	TEAM	REBOUNDS	ASSISTS	STEALS	POINTS
4	Georgetown	6.4	2.4	1.5	15.3

NBA

GAMES	TEAM	REBOUNDS	ASSISTS	STEALS	POINTS
419	Denver	4.6	2.9	1.5	14.2
103	Los Angeles (LAC)	3.0	1.7	1.2	10.4
32	Cleveland	1.9	1.2	0.7	6.8
32	San Antonio	2.1	1.6	0.7	6.7
11	New Jersey	2.2	0.7	0.7	6.5
2	Indiana	3.5	1.0	0.0	2.5

David Wingate Career Stats, Per Game

COLLEGE

YEARS	TEAM	REBOUNDS	ASSISTS	STEALS	POINTS
4	Georgetown	3.6	2.6	1.5	12.8

NBA

GAMES	TEAM	REBOUNDS	ASSISTS	STEALS	POINTS
184	Seattle	1.1	1.0	0.5	3.3
174	Charlotte	2.1	2.0	0.7	5.0
171	Philadelphia	1.7	2.0	0.9	8.0
103	San Antonio	2.6	2.5	1.0	6.4
81	Washington	3.3	3.0	1.5	7.9
27	New York	0.4	0.3	0.2	0.6

Source: basketballreference.com

ACKNOWLEDGMENTS

THIS BOOK WOULD NOT have been possible without the unconditional love and unwavering support of my mother, Mariana Danois. We didn't have much when I was growing up, but she managed to make me feel like the richest kid in the world.

My daughters Maia Linda Danois and Laila Assata Danois have been an unbelievable source of motivation and inspiration. Thanks, girls.

Ericka Blount Danois, you are beyond amazing.

To the best mentor and friend that anyone could ever ask for, Garry D. Howard, who changed my life when he decided to take me under his wing. And his lovely wife, Donna, whose delicious food and hospitality brought warmth into my life when it was most needed.

Special thanks to my dad as well, David Danois, who taught me, through his personal example, about putting your heart and soul into your passion. Much love to Cindy Danois and my sisters Danielle, Alana, Melissa, and Cristina as well.

To my brother, Derek Danois, and his awesome wife, Diane,

for showing me that the combination of drive, talent, and persistence is unbeatable.

This project would never have gotten off the ground without Bob Wade trusting me with his story. Thanks, Coach, and your lovely wife, Carolyn, for inviting me into your home, your life, and the Dunbar family.

To my friend Sherron Bogues, your loss is felt by the many lives you touched here in Baltimore.

To the incomparable Tyrone "Muggsy" Bogues, who is perhaps the greatest underdog success story in the history of sports. Thanks for opening up your home to me and being passionate about this project.

Also, to one of the coolest guys I know, Reggie Williams, for always picking up the phone and putting the time aside to share his thoughts and insights about a time in his life that he cherishes.

And to all of the Poets and members of the Dunbar and Baltimore basketball family who met with me, sat for long phone and in-person interviews, participated in the conference calls, and helped the great history of the school and city come alive to re-create the 1981–1982 season: Lynn Badham, Keith Wallace, Karl Wallace, Darryl "OJ" Wood, Marshall Goodwin, Tim Dawson, Ellis Dawson, Ernie Graham, Gary Graham, Skip Wise, Leon Howard, Carl Fair, Eric Green, the Poet Followers, David Wingate, Mike Brown, Preston Jay, Keith Mills, Anthony "Dudie" Lewis, Chuckie Bogues, Jerry White, and so many others.

To Herman "Tree" Harried, who was a powerful force behind the scenes of this project whose door was always open. Thanks, Tree.

To my friend and former Milton Academy schoolmate Touré, who was a tremendous help, sharing his valuable insights and constructive criticisms when I began bouncing this idea off him over ten years ago.

I will forever be indebted to *Sports Illustrated*'s Chris Hunt, who encouraged me when this idea was merely in its embryonic stage, and who ultimately advised the literary agents at Inkwell Management to reach out to me.

Thanks to Tom Jolly at the *New York Times*, for believing in my storytelling abilities.

To Sam Davis at the *Baltimore Sun* and Randy Harvey at the *Houston Chronicle*, for their great advice and mentorship over the years. Special shout-out to Lem Satterfield, Gary Adornato, and Derek Toney as well.

Thanks to Rod Stokes, Latanya Stokes, Kwame Rich, Carlos Rice, and the entire Regeneration Project family.

And to my friend Steve Vassor, along with the great folks at the Hampden Family Center—Lisa Ghinger, Pam Viel, Alice-Ann Finnerty, Tom Finnerty, and all of the staff, kids, families, and board members.

I would like to thank all of the great teachers who lit a spark in me. Mr. Lefkowitz at P.S. 346 in Brooklyn; Mark Hilgendorf, Jim Conolly, Randy McCutcheon, Roger Connor, and John Banderob at Milton Academy; and the late Professor Kristin Hunter Lattany at the University of Pennsylvania all changed my life, giving me the keys that would open up my mind and my life.

To the English and Language Skills Departments at Milton Academy, thank you for making me fall in love with the majesty, power, and beauty of the written word.

To my best friend, peer mentor, and brother from another mother, Maurice Plaines, who has had my back since childhood. Love you, man.

And to my childhood buddies Lonnie Hart, Dexter Fairclough,

Erik Lawrence, and Craig Hillman, I doubt there were many kids who had more fun and laughs than we did.

To my New York City public school crew—Danny Santiago, Sebastian Marquez, Brian Yoon, Tara Texiera, and LaTonya Minor, I appreciate you guys. I'm still laughing at some of the shenanigans.

Special thanks to all of the great coaches I had growing up, especially Tom Flaherty and Nathan Taylor at Milton. I appreciate you guys.

Fran McGinnis, who provided a daily dose of much-needed motherly love in the Milton activities office: you were awesome.

To Mr. and Mrs. Foley and the entire Foley family, thanks for allowing me to have a real home away from home, and for keeping the fridge stocked with cold cuts. I'm proud to call you guys my adopted Irish family.

To the young men of Wolcott House who became my brothers, along with our dorm parents and advisers.

I am forever indebted to the amazing Keisha McClellan, who was the first person to tell me that I was a writer back in 1984, and to Dean Garfield, who has been a brother to me since the days of daydreaming in Wolcott House and the endless hours shooting hoops in the Saltonstall Gymnasium. I love you guys.

To Mr. Neville Lake, who took a chance on a poor kid from Brooklyn, and Brian Cirksey, Drake Holliday, Valeriani Bead, Dorado Kinney, Cliff "Da Knife" Evans, Frances Santiago, Elizabeth Hexner, Jenna Moscowitz, Mike Foley, Touré, Jason Downie, Joe Kolton, Mark "Cookie" Simmons, Duburne Helwig Nehemiah Darius Reid, Brendan Garvey, Patrice Jean-Baptiste, Debbie Cardoza, Joel Del Rosario, Aisha Harris, Annie Elliot, Curt Cetrulo, Katy Henrickson, Marc Goodman, Maurice Lee, Taylor Fogelquist, Tim Sullivan, Ron Nickens, Darryl Kirton,

Sara Colt, David Abaire, Carla Burton, Jacky Simmonds, Dan Hermann, Sarah Sze, Dana Jackson, Rob Azeke, Lamont Gordon, J. R. Torrico, Jose Robledo, and all of the other brilliant, hilarious folks from Milton who impacted me in such a profound way, thank you.

To my Andover, Exeter, and St. Paul's crew, with a special shout-out to the NEALSA party overnights in prep school.

To my INROADS folks, especially the lovely Lyssa Morris. Those Wall Street internship lunch dates were among the highlights of my college summers.

To all of my extraordinary peers at the University of Pennsylvania and the extended network at Drexel and Villanova, thanks to John Pembroke, Walt Frazier III, Stu Fisher, Kenny Fikes, Sean Jodi Diaz, Charles Adams, Jerome Palmore, Ryan Harris, Harlan Taylor, Hassan Duncombe, Rich Gadsby, Mike Persaud, Jon Essoka, Jeff Gordon, Steve Alvarado, Taliba Foster, Kysha Harris, Avis Kinnard, Collette Ramsey, Don Hatter, Doug Glanville, Ayanna Taylor-Venson, Karen Wright-Sanders, Shareese De Vose, Carol Santos, Stephanie Grimes, Rhonda Anderson, Rachel Herbert, Stacey Conner, Laurene Williams, Karen Wright Sanders, Dana Baxter, Christine Bussey, Natacha Baron, Rich Gay, Thyme Gadson, and so many others. You guys made Penn the place to be!

To the fantastic Shanda Hall, who is one of the most awesome, genuine people I've ever met.

Special thanks to Kurt Collier, Dr. Patricia Turner, and Dr. Inez Felicia Adams, whose hilarity, love, backing, and support walked me through the writing of this book, from the first word to the last.

To my college mentor, Mr. Harold Haskins: your voice and words still resonate today. Thanks so much for your wisdom and interest in me.

To my Mighty Psi Chapter brothers of Alpha Phi Alpha: Curtis Myers, Derrick Melvin, Geoffrey Cousins, Roberto Vargas, Franklin Ferguson Jr., Rod Teachey, Eric Apple, Derek McEwen, Tom Driver, Ramon Jones, Alvin Bowman, Eric Smith, Ricco Keyes, Melvin Steals, Lawrence Leonard, Mark Ball, Alexis Jones, Preston Thompson, Scott Kemp, David France, Grant Davis, Tom Wilson, Elliot Peters, Garrick Francis, Kevin Raiford, Scott King, Bryan Keys, Perry Fergus, Marc Palmer, Marvin "the Jewel" Lyon, Travis Jackson, Lynch Hunt, Eric Williams, Sean Gumbs, Marcus Chapman, Devon Sanders, Tony Frazier, Stan Bradford, Damon Green, Malaney Hill, Mike Rodgers, Bill Roberts, Dave Sterling, Andre Wade, Damon Manning, Clarence Armstrong, Wayne Wilson, Kris Love, Moses Hart, Mitch Lucas, and everyone else I forgot to mention, along with those who came before and after us. Manly deeds, scholarship, and love for all mankind. College days swiftly pass, but our bonds of brotherhood will last a lifetime.

To my grandparents Christina Baez, Juan Baez, Ana Danois, and Sixto Danois. Words could never express what you guys gave me.

To Patricia Ham, Gary Ham, and the entire Ham family: love you guys. Thanks to all of my aunts and uncles—Rosie, Millie, Eleana, Damaris, Larry, Butch, Lino, Sixto, and Mary, along with all of my cousins.

Big shout-out to my Falero family and a special thanks to my first athletic and life role models, my cousins Darrell and Donald Jones.

To the oasis—Cambridge Place between Gates and Greene Avenues—and the basketball courts at P.S. 11, Tillary Park, Rucker, West Fourth, P.S. 20, F3, and Emerson Park.

To my cherished aunt and mentor Andrea Cisco, along with Chris Cisco, the entire Cisco family, Bob House, Patricia House,

Mark House, and the Mayor of Greene Avenue in Brooklyn, Bill Clinton. Thanks for everything.

Aunt Clara, thanks for always being a shoulder to lean on. Jonai, you are loved and terribly missed.

To my LEAD Program at Wharton peers—Joel Harris, Darnell Moore, Terri Stroud, Matt Barnhill, April Lewis, and everyone else—what a magical summer that was back in 1987.

To the Warlord Saleem and the S.S. think tank. The brains, hilarity, and creativity never cease to amaze me.

To Keith Clinkscales, Yussuf Khan, and the entire team at The Shadow League: thanks for allowing me to tell the stories that I'm passionate about.

To my New York City basketball family, especially my cousins Tarik Campbell and Gary Campbell, along with Sean Couch, Jesse Washington, Mike Parker, Bobbito Garcia, and Terrence Watson.

To Bobby Sabelhaus, aka "Sabelhorn!," Sheldon Candis, and Eric Levy, for helping me take things to an entirely different level.

Jerry Bembry, Sunni Khalid, and David Steele, you guys are outstanding friends, peer mentors, and role models.

Special thanks to George Raveling.

To the entire Blount/Berry gang—Elissa, Linda, Walter, Lew, Faith, Jomo, Sunny, and Ziggy. I love and appreciate you guys.

To my beautiful friend Nichole Brathwaite-Dingle, who has been in my corner for over twenty-five years.

Much love to Daphne Dufresne, Carol Dufresne, Mama Dufresne, and Joe Amprey for lighting up my daughters' lives and for the continued support.

And to the late, great Jeffrey Mark Dingle: words can't express my gratitude. I'm a better man because of you. I miss you, brother.

I have been blessed with the most awesome literary agent that anyone could ask for, the very cool, incredibly brilliant Ethan Bassoff at Lippincott Massie McQuilkin. Thanks, my man. I'm lucky to call you not only my agent, but my friend. Looking forward to building a library together, my man.

I've also been fortunate to have worked with Bob Bender on this book. His ability to pull it out of me, as I reflect on early drafts of this book, was beyond amazing. I'm so lucky to have been given the opportunity to work with and learn from him, along with his assistant, Johanna Li, and all of the wonderful folks at Simon & Schuster. Special thanks to Tim Gay for helping me to bring the manuscript down the homestretch, and for our meetings with the great food at Miss Shirley's. It really has been a dream come true. I look forward to doing more work together in the days and years ahead.

INDEX